Editor
Kim Fields

Managing Editor
Ina Massler Levin, M.A.

Editor-in-Chief
Sharon Coan, M.S. Ed.

Cover Art
Barb Lorseyedi

Art Manager
Kevin Barnes

Art Director
CJae Froshay

Imaging
Rosa C. See

Product Manager
Phil Garcia

Ideas contributed by
Jeanne Dustman, M.Ed.
Maureen Gerard, Ph.D.

Publishers
Rachelle Cracchiolo, M.S. Ed.
Mary Dupuy Smith, M.S. Ed.

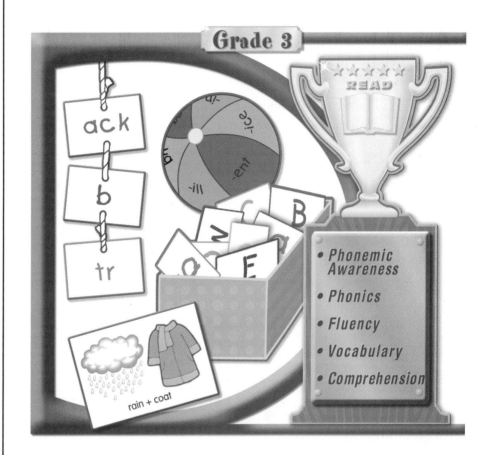

Grade 3

- *Phonemic Awareness*
- *Phonics*
- *Fluency*
- *Vocabulary*
- *Comprehension*

rain + coat

Author

Jennifer Overend Prior, Ph.D.

Teacher Created Materials, Inc.
6421 Industry Way
Westminster, CA 92683
www.teachercreated.com
ISBN-0-7439-3023-1
©2004 Teacher Created Materials, Inc.
Made in U.S.A.

Table of Contents

Introduction

More than ever before, children's development of reading skills has come to the forefront of education in the United States. The National Reading Panel (2000) presented a report entitled, "Teaching Children to Read: An Evidence-Based Assessment of the Scientific Research Literature on Reading and Its Implications for Reading Instruction—Reports of Subgroups." This report reflects reading research, focusing on kindergarten through grade three, and targets methods of instruction that lead to reading success. The panel's report highlights the following elements of reading:

✧ **Phonemic Awareness**   ✧ **Vocabulary**

✧ **Phonics**   ✧ **Comprehension**

✧ **Fluency**

This book provides teachers with practical strategies for teaching reading skills in these areas.

The terminology below is commonly used when discussing reading instruction and will be helpful in understanding and discussing the five elements of reading.

✧ General Terminology

- **explicit instruction**—direct instruction of strategies by the teacher

- **implicit instruction**—indirect instruction, often embedded in context

✧ Phonemic Awareness

- **phonemic awareness**—an individual's ability to attend to the sounds of spoken words

- **phonological awareness**—ability to recognize phonemes, graphemes, rhymes, syllables, etc.

- **phonemes**—sounds in spoken language

- **graphemes**—the smallest part of written language

- **phonics**—relationship between the sounds and symbols of spoken and written language

- **syllable**—part of a word that contains a vowel or vowel sound

- **onset**—the initial consonant in a syllable

- **rime**—the syllable part that contains a vowel
  (Example: In *dog*, the onset is *d*, and the rime is *og*.)

Introduction *(cont.)*

✧ **Phonics**

- **synthetic phonics**—the ability to convert letters into sounds and blend them together
- **analytic phonics**—the ability to analyze the letters and sounds in words
- **analogy-based phonics**—using knowledge of word families to read unfamiliar words
- **phonics through spelling**—the ability to break words into sounds for writing
- **embedded phonics**—the instruction of letters and sounds within text
- **onset-rime phonics**—instruction that involves the identification of the initial sound in a word part (onset) and the remaining part of the word (rime)

✧ **Fluency**

- **fluency**—reading quickly and accurately
- **automaticity**—the quick recognition of words

✧ **Vocabulary**

- **specific-word instruction**—the teaching of individual words
- **word-learning strategies**—the instruction of strategies that help children determine word meaning
- **word parts**—using parts of words (prefixes, suffixes, base words) to determine meanings of words
- **context clues**—surrounding phrases, sentences, and words that provide hints that lead to a word's meaning

✧ **Comprehension**

- **metacognition**—thinking about one's thinking or the ability to identify what is known and not known when reading
- **semantic organizers**—maps or webs used to illustrate the connection between concepts or ideas
- **direct explanation**—a teacher's explanation of the use of comprehension strategies
- **modeling**—teacher demonstration of the use of strategies
- **guided practice**—guidance by the teacher as a student applies strategies
- **application**—student practice of reading strategies

This book is divided into five sections featuring each of the elements of reading. Within each section you'll find activities for teacher-directed instruction as well as small group and individual practice of reading skills. Many of the activities include follow-up games and reproducibles intended to provide additional practice of skills. The use of these activities, games, and practice sheets added to your comprehensive reading program will give your students the necessary skills for reading success.

Meeting Reading Standards

The chart below and on pages 6–7 displays the McREL standards for reading in grades 3–5. Used with permission from McREL (copyright 2000 McREL, Mid-continent Research for Education and Learning, 2550 S. Parker Road, Suite 500, Aurora, CO 80014. Telephone: 303-337-0990. Web site: *www.mcrel.org/standards-benchmarks)*. The checks indicate the standards that are addressed by activities in this book. You will see a standards/objectives citation below each activity in the book.

Standard 5: Uses the general skills and strategies of the reading process	
1. Previews text (e.g., skims material; uses pictures, textual clues, and text format)	√
2. Establishes a purpose for reading (e.g., for information, for pleasure, to understand a specific viewpoint)	√
3. Represents concrete information (e.g., persons, places, things, events) as explicit mental pictures	
4. Makes, confirms, and revises simple predictions about what will be found in a text (e.g., uses prior knowledge and ideas presented in text, illustrations, titles, topic sentences, key words, and foreshadowing clues)	
5. Uses phonetic and structural analysis techniques, syntactic structure, and semantic context to decode unknown words (e.g., vowel patterns, complex word families, syllabication, root words, affixes)	√
6. Uses a variety of context clues to decode unknown words (e.g., draws on earlier reading, reads ahead)	√
7. Uses word reference materials (e.g., glossary, dictionary, thesaurus) to determine the meaning, pronunciation, and derivations of unknown words	√
8. Understands level-appropriate reading vocabulary (e.g., synonyms, antonyms, homophones, multi-meaning words)	√
9. Monitors own reading strategies and makes modifications as needed (e.g., recognizes when he or she is confused by a section of text; questions whether the text makes sense)	√
10. Adjusts speed of reading to suit purpose and difficulty of the material	√
11. Understands the author's purpose (e.g., to persuade, to inform)	
12. Uses personal criteria to select reading material (e.g., personal interest, knowledge of authors and genres, text difficulty, recommendations of others)	√

Meeting Reading Standards *(cont.)*

The chart below is a continuation of the chart on page 5 that displays the McREL standards for reading in grades 3–5. The checks indicate the standards that are addressed by activities in this book. You will see a standards/objectives citation below each activity in the book.

Standard 6: Uses reading skills and strategies to understand and interpret a variety of literary text	
1. Uses reading skills and strategies to understand a variety of literary passages and texts (e.g., fairy tales, folktales, fiction, nonfiction, myths, poems, fables, fantasies, historical fiction, biographies, autobiographies, chapter books)	
2. Knows the defining characteristics of a variety of literary forms and genres (e.g., fairy tales, folktales, fiction, nonfiction, myths, poems, fables, fantasies, historical fiction, biographies, autobiographies, chapter books)	
3. Understands the basic concept of plot (e.g., main problem, conflict, resolution, cause-and-effect)	√
4. Understands similarities and differences within and among literary works from various genres and cultures (e.g., in terms of settings, character types, events, point of view; role of natural phenomena)	√
5. Understands elements of character development in literary works (e.g., differences between main and minor characters; stereotypical characters as opposed to fully developed characters; changes that characters undergo; the importance of a character's actions, motives, and appearance to plot and theme)	√
6. Makes inferences or draws conclusions about characters' qualities and actions (e.g., based on knowledge of plot, setting, characters' motives, characters' appearances, other characters' responses to a character)	√
7. Knows themes that recur across literary works	
8. Understands the ways in which language is used in literary texts (e.g., personification, alliteration, onomatopoeia, simile, metaphor, imagery, hyperbole, beat, rhythm)	
9. Makes connections between characters or simple events in a literary work and people or events in his or her own life	√

Meeting Reading Standards *(cont.)*

The chart below is a continuation of the chart on page 6 that displays the McREL standards for reading in grades 3–5. The checks indicate the standards that are addressed by activities in this book. You will see a standards/objectives citation below each activity in the book.

Standard 7: Uses reading skills and strategies to understand and interpret a variety of informational texts	
1. Uses reading skills and strategies to understand a variety of informational texts (e.g., textbooks, biographical sketches, letters, diaries, directions, procedures, magazines)	
2. Knows the defining characteristics of a variety of informational texts (e.g., textbooks, biographical sketches, letters, diaries, directions, procedures, magazines)	
3. Uses text organizers (e.g., headings, topic and summary sentences, graphic features, typeface, chapter titles) to determine the main ideas and to locate information in a text	√
4. Uses the various parts of a book (e.g., index, table of contents, glossary, appendix, preface) to locate information	
5. Summarizes and paraphrases information in texts (e.g., includes the main idea and significant supporting details of a reading selection)	√
6. Uses prior knowledge and experience to understand and respond to new information	√
7. Understands the author's viewpoint in an informational text	
8. Understands structural patterns or organization in informational texts (e.g., chronological, logical, or sequential order; compare-and-contrast; cause-and-effect; proposition and support)	√

Phonemic Awareness

Phonemic awareness refers to an individual's ability to attend to the sounds of spoken words. In order to begin to read, a child needs to understand that words are made up of individual sounds. It is important to remember that phonemic awareness activities should be fun and playful for the children.

Why Teach Phonemic Awareness?

Research suggests that experience with and instruction of phonemic awareness benefits children in their quest to become readers. Phonemic awareness assists children in spelling and should be related to letters in order to assist them with transitioning from hearing sounds to reading words.

You will notice that this section of the book is somewhat shorter than the others, as most children in third grade have already developed phonemic awareness. It is likely, however, that some of your students will still need practice in this area, which is why these activities have been included. You may want to incorporate these playful activities as a part of a whole class routine.

As described in the report of The National Reading Panel, there are several elements involved in phonemic awareness instruction. These include phoneme isolation, phoneme identity, phoneme categorization, phoneme blending, phoneme segmentation, phoneme deletion, phoneme addition, and phoneme substitution.

- ➤ **Phoneme Isolation** (recognizing sounds in words)
  - Example: The first sound in *dog* is /d/.
- ➤ **Phoneme Identity** (recognizing words that have similar sounds)
  - Example: The words *cat, car,* and *cave* all begin with /c/.
- ➤ **Phoneme Categorization** (recognizing words that sound the same and words that sound different)
  - Example: The words *bun, run,* and *fun* have similar sounds. The word *bat* does not sound the same.
- ➤ **Phoneme Blending** (combining spoken phonemes into words)
  - Example: The sounds /t//u//g/ make the word *tug*.
- ➤ **Phoneme Segmentation** (breaking words into their separate phonemes)
  - Example: There are four sounds in the word *truck* (/t/ /r/ /u/ /k/).
- ➤ **Phoneme Deletion** (identifying a new word when a phoneme is removed from another word)
  - Example: If you take away the /s/ in *start*, you have the word *tart*.
- ➤ **Phoneme Addition** (identifying a new word when a phoneme is added to another word)
  - Example: If you add /s/ to the beginning of *port*, you have the word *sport*.
- ➤ **Phoneme Substitution** (changing a phoneme in a word to make a new word)
  - Example: If you change the /p/ in *cap* to /t/, you have the word *cat*.

When facilitating phonemic awareness activities, focus only on one or two of these elements at a time. Keep in mind, also, that you may teach phonemic awareness in a variety of formats—whole group, small group, or individual instruction. You will need to determine which format best suits the needs of your students.

Phoneme Isolation Activities

Phoneme isolation is the ability to recognize the sounds in words.

The End of a Name

Standard: 5.1

Materials

- none required

1. For this game, explain to the children that they will listen for the sounds at the ends of their names.
2. Gather your students together.
3. Ask each child to tell the sound that is heard at the end of his or her name. *Jaden* ends with the /n/ sound.
4. After students identify the sounds at the ends of their names, instruct them to organize themselves into groups based on these sounds. For example, all of the students with /a/ at the ends of their names stand together.
5. Be sure to discuss the fact that some names end with the same sound, but do not contain the same letter. For example, *Jodi* and *Cathy* end with the same sound, but the letters are different.

Extension: To associate letter sounds with letter symbols, create lists of students' names that end with the same sounds. You might also want to do the same with the names' beginning letters.

Do You Hear What I Hear?

Standard: 5.1

Materials

- none required

1. Ask students to listen for vowel sounds they hear in the middle of words.
2. Begin by saying a word, such as *bun*. Ask the students, "What vowel sound do you hear in the middle of *bun*?"
3. Emphasize the sound as you say it for students who need assistance.
4. Continue this activity by saying two or three words with the same middle vowel sound, such as *tag, mat, tap*. Ask the question, "What vowel sound do you hear in the middle of these words?" See below for groups of words to use for practice.

Words with /a/ in the middle	**Words with /e/ in the middle**	**Words with /ee/ in the middle**
trap blast nab	get bend sell	keep treat heel

Words with /i/ in the middle	**Words with /oa/ in the middle**	**Words with /u/ in the middle**
sit trip flinch	boat foam rode	mud truck love

Phoneme Identity Activities

Phoneme identity is the ability to recognize that some words contain the same sounds. To increase the difficulty of this skill for third graders, focus on combinations of letters, such as blends, double vowels, "r"-controlled vowels, etc.

Listen Up!

Standard: 5.1

Materials

- none required

1. Gather students together. Explain that you will say three words. Their job is to determine which blend sound is the same in each word.
2. Begin by saying three words with the same beginning blend sound, such as *trap, treat*, and *try*. After students identify that each word has the /tr/ blend sound, ask them to try to identify the two letters that make that sound.
3. Try this with several groups of words with the same beginning blend sound.
4. Make the activity more challenging by saying groups of words with the same double vowels, or "r"-controlled vowels. See below for groups of words.

Same Blend Sounds

glass, glow, glitch   bread, break, brown   slide, slick, slime

grain, grease, grime   blow, blonde, blame   stick, stay, staff

train, truck, tram

Same Double Vowel Sound

heat, feast, cream

piece, niece, shield

coat, float, foam

Same Digraphs

ship, shore, shelf

champ, chill, chunk

brush, sash, mush

crunch, lunch, much

Same "r"-Controlled Vowel Sound

hurt, slurp, turn   shirt, first, firm   germ, fern, stern

cart, farm, tarp   fort, horn, fork

Phoneme Identity Activities *(cont.)*

What Do You Hear?

Standard: 5.1

This activity will help your students identify the different sounds made by letters of the alphabet.

Materials

- index cards
- marker
- shoebox

1. With a marker, write each letter of the alphabet on a different index card.
2. Place the cards in a shoebox. In turn, invite each student to select a card from the box.
3. Have each child think of the different sounds that can be made by the letter.
4. Ask each student to pronounce the sounds aloud. Allow classmates to offer assistance, if necessary.
5. To make the activity more challenging, ask the students to think of words that display the different letter sounds.

> Example:
> The letter **a** makes different sounds in words, such as *bag* and *cake*.
> The letter **g** makes a hard sound in *get* and a soft sound in *gentle*.

Phoneme by Phoneme

Standard: 5.1

This activity will provide your students with practice identifying phonemes.

Materials

- magazines
- scissors
- glue
- index cards

1. Prepare for this activity by gluing a different magazine picture on each index card.
2. Place the index cards in a learning center.
3. To play, a student selects a card and says the name of the picture on it.
4. Then the student pronounces the picture name again separating it phoneme by phoneme, rather than saying the whole word. For example, a student might say *tree*, /t/ /r/ /ee/.
5. The student continues in this manner until all of the pictures have been named.
6. Extend this activity by providing more index cards, magazines, glue, and scissors in the learning center.
7. The student locates other appealing pictures to cut out and glue on index cards. These cards are added to the stack for other students to use as they participate in the learning center activity.

Phoneme Categorization Activities

Phoneme categorization is the ability to recognize words that sound the same and different.

Which Word Doesn't Belong?

Standard: 5.1

Materials

• none required

1. For this activity, your students will be asked to identify the word in a set of three that does not sound the same as the others.

2. Say the words *bun, fun,* and *cake.* Ask the students to identify which word does not belong.

3. Ask the students to explain why the word is different. Try this activity with rhyming words as well as with words that have same and different beginning and ending sounds.

4. To make the activity more challenging, have your students listen for similar and different blends. See below for sample word groups.

Rhyming/Not Rhyming	**Beginning Sound**	**Blends**
try, fly, wake	candle, light, came	snake, snail, slide
coat, float, trick	funny, many, miner	treat, trick, tail
make, sit, mitt	house, hat, shower	glow, green, gram
stable, cable, ready	kitchen, kite, fish	brow, brick, blow

Sound Categorization

Standard: 5.1

This learning center activity provides your students with ongoing practice of categorizing sounds in words.

Materials

• cards on pages 13–14   • scissors   • resealable plastic bags

1. Have your students practice phoneme categorization at a learning center.

2. Duplicate the cards on pages 13–14 and cut them out.

3. Color the cards and laminate them for durability.

4. Create sets of three cards. Place each set in a resealable plastic bag. Place the bags at the learning center.

5. To play, a child takes the cards out of a bag, reads the words, and determines which words have the same sounds and which word is different.

6. Have the child identify how the words are the same and different.

7. The child continues in this manner with each set of words. Encourage children to work together to assess one another's progress.

Categorization Cards

strong	**wrong**
ring	**trip**
flip	**map**
funny	**bunny**
chilly	**chair**
hair	**far**

Categorization Cards *(cont.)*

roar	rage
gain	cloud
clay	cry
fan	run
game	brush
trash	crutch

Phoneme Blending Activities

Phoneme blending is the ability to combine spoken phonemes into words.

I'm Thinking of . . .

Standard: 5.1

Materials

- none required

1. For this activity, your students will need to listen to a set of sounds and determine which word you have in mind.
2. Think of a word and say the separate sounds that make up the word, such as /t/ /a/ /b/ /l/.
3. The students listen to the sounds and combine them to make the word *table*.
4. Begin by using two-syllable words and increase the difficulty with three-syllable words. (See below.)
5. Allow the students to think of their own words to share with the class in the same manner.
6. As the length of the words increase, students may experience more difficulty blending the sounds into words. To assist them, say the first few sounds and have the students blend them together. Then say the next few sounds and have the students blend them together and add them to the first part of the word.

Extension: Extend this activity by separating the names of students.

Two-Syllable Words
happy /h//a//p//ee/
hamster /h//a//m//s//t//r/
baby /b//a//b//ee/
summer /s//u//m//r/
notebook /n//o//t//b//u//k/

Three-Syllable Words
yesterday /y//e//s//t//r//d//a/
tornado /t//o//r//n//a//d//o/
holiday /h//o//l//i/d//a/
abandon /u//b//a//n//d//u//n/
basketball /b//a//s//k//e//t//b//a//l/

Listen to the Sounds

Standard: 5.1

Materials

- none required

1. Similar to the activity above, invite students to select their own words.
2. After each student thinks of a word, have him or her say the word slowly to determine the individual sounds.
3. Invite each student, in turn, to say each sound in the word as classmates try to guess the word.

Phoneme Segmentation Activities

Phoneme segmentation is the ability to break words into their separate phonemes.

Say and Spell

Standard: 5.1

This activity will help children use sound identification to spell words in their independent writing.

Materials

- chart paper
- marker
- paper
- pencils

1. Gather selected students together at a table and provide each with paper and pencil.
2. Say a word and discuss the individual sounds they hear in the word.
3. Demonstrate how to write the word phonetically based on the sounds they hear. Write the phonetic spelling on chart paper. (If you feel these students are ready for the challenge, ask them to examine the phonetic spelling and make changes to the word to bring it closer to its conventional spelling.)
4. Instruct the students to try this on their own. Be sure to assist students who have difficulty.
5. You may feel uncomfortable leaving words in their phonetic form, but helping your students to use invented spelling will assist them in their independent writing. This will lead to an increased ability to spell conventionally over time.

Sound It Out

Standards: 5.1, 5.5

This activity will help a student become aware of individual sounds while writing independently.

Materials

- word cards (pages 18–19)
- paper and pencils

1. Duplicate the deletion word cards on pages 18–19.
2. Gather selected students at a table.
3. Choose a word card and say the first sound of the word.
4. Ask students what letter makes that sound.
5. Then have each student write down the first sound on his or her paper.
6. Repeat the activity until each sound in the word has been said and written. Choose another word and continue in the same manner.

Phoneme Deletion Activities

Phoneme deletion is the ability to identify a new word when a phoneme is removed from another word.

Remove It

Standard: 5.1

This activity encourages your students to be sound detectives.

Materials

- none required

1. Say a word and then ask the children to determine what the word would change to if a sound is removed. For example, "What word is left if we remove the /s/ from *smile*?" (*mile*)

2. Continue in this manner. A list of these word changes is provided below.

> What word is left if we remove the /s/ from *scare?* (*care*)
>
> What word is left if we remove the /b/ from *blend?* (*lend*)
>
> What word is left if we remove the /t/ from *tray?* (*ray*)
>
> What word is left if we remove the /a/ from *around?* (*round*)
>
> What word is left if we remove the /s/ from *slip?* (*lip*)
>
> What word is left if we remove the /c/ from *crate?* (*rate*)
>
> What word is left if we remove the /l/ from *bushel?* (*bush*)
>
> What word is left if we remove the /p/ from *plate?* (*late*)
>
> What word is left if we remove the /k/ from *scat?* (*sat*)

Deletion Cards

Standard: 5.1

Use this activity to allow your children to practice phoneme deletion independently.

Materials

- copies of deletion cards on pages 18–19
- scissors

1. Duplicate the word cards on pages 18–19. Laminate the cards and cut them apart.

2. You will notice that each card has one or two dots above and below the word. The dots indicate places where the card can be folded backward to delete a letter.

3. The student's job is to read the original word and then determine the word that will remain when the first or last sound is removed.

4. As an added challenge, ask students to determine if more than one letter on the card could be deleted to make yet another word. (This works with some, but not all, of the words.)

Deletion Cards

• **s u p p e r** •	• **f a l l** •
• **b r e e d** •	• • **s l a t e** • •
• **g l o w** •	• **b l o c k** •
• **s h a p e** •	• • **t r a c e** • •
• **s p o i l** •	• **d e a r** •

Deletion Cards *(cont.)*

c a r t	h a n d y
b e a t e r	b o w l
s i l l y	f i r m
f o r k	l a w n
h a n d l e	y e l l o w

Phoneme Addition & Substitution Activities

Phoneme addition refers to the identification of a new word when a phoneme is added to another word.

Add Ons

Standard: 5.1

With this phoneme addition activity, your students will be challenged to determine new words when letters are added to shorter words.

Materials

- none required

1. Begin by saying a word such as *plan*. Then ask how the word would change if the letter **t** were to be added to the end. Help the students to see that *plan* becomes *plant* when the **t** is added.
2. Continue in this manner with the words listed below. Allow the children to create some of their own phoneme additions.
3. Be sure to challenge the students by adding letters to the beginnings and endings of words. Use the lists below to help you.

Ending Additions	
fin /ch/	tram /p/
cloud /y/	pest /r/
car /t/	

Beginning Additions	
/a/ round	/s/ lip
/s/ cold	/d/ rag
/t/ rap	

Phoneme substitution refers to the ability to change a phoneme in a word to make a new word.

Make the Switch

Standard: 5.1

Phoneme substitution is similar to phoneme addition, but in this activity students determine a new word that is made by changing one or two letters in an existing word.

Materials

- none required

1. Begin by saying a word such as *table*.
2. Ask how the word would change if the /t/ sound was changed to the /k/ sound (*table* becomes *cable*).
3. Continue in this manner with the words listed in the box. Feel free to substitute more than one letter when using blends.
4. Allow the children to create some of their own phoneme substitutions.

brick/click
weather/heather
tree/free
tumble/fumble
brown/frown
skill/skip
paper/pager

Change the Sound

What happens when you change a sound in a word to another sound? Discover each new word below.

1. Change the /j/ in *just* to /m/. The new word is _____.

2. Change the /t/ in *too* to /z/. The new word is _____.

3. Change the /m/ in *mix* to /f/. The new word is _____.

4. Change the /d/ in *lead* to /p/. The new word is _____.

5. Change the /n/ in *sharpen* to /r/. The new word is _____.

6. Change the /c/ in *crown* to /f/. The new word is _____.

7. Change the /h/ in *handle* to /c/. The new word is _____.

8. Change the /j/ in *jeep* to /k/. The new word is _____.

9. Change the /h/ in *heater* to /ch/. The new word is _____.

10. Change the /sc/ in *scatter* to /ch/. The new word is _____.

Change one letter in each word below. Write the new word on the line.

1. down _____

2. car_____

3. camp_____

4. game_____

5. trick_____

Phonemic Awareness Four-Point Rubric

Use the rubric below to score a student's phonemic awareness skills in the following areas:

- ✧ phoneme isolation
- ✧ phoneme identity
- ✧ phoneme categorization
- ✧ phoneme blending
- ✧ phoneme segmentation
- ✧ phoneme deletion
- ✧ phoneme addition
- ✧ phoneme substitution

Student Name: _____

Date: _____

Points	Description
4	The student has a thorough understanding of all areas of phonemic awareness.
3	The student has a solid understanding of six or seven areas of phonemic awareness.
2	The student has an understanding of four or five areas of phonemic awareness.
1	The student struggles in four or more areas of phonemic awareness.

Comments:

_____

_____

_____

_____

_____

Phonics

As a result of the debate between phonics and whole-language, phonics instruction has become a controversial issue with many educators. Phonics instruction is not intended to be the sole method of reading instruction. Phonics skills do, however, help children learn the relationships between the letters of written language and the sounds of spoken language. This leads to an understanding of the alphabetic principle.

Why Teach Phonics?

Phonics instruction is important because it improves:

- children's word recognition and spelling in kindergarten and first grade
- reading comprehension
- the skills of children with reading difficulties

In order for phonics instruction to be most effective, it should be introduced early in the school experience. As mentioned earlier, phonics instruction should not be the entire focus of a reading program, but rather an important part of a well-balanced program.

As described in the report of The National Reading Panel, there are several approaches to phonics instruction. Some educators use one approach exclusively, while others use a combination of approaches. These approaches are described below:

- **Synthetic Phonics**—children learn to convert letters into sounds, blending the sounds together to form recognizable words.
- **Analytic Phonics**—children analyze letter-sound relationships in words they have already learned. Sounds are not taught or pronounced in isolation.
- **Analogy-Based Phonics**—children identify new words by using what they know about parts of word families.
- **Phonics through Spelling**—children break words into individual sounds and write words by identifying each phoneme and writing a letter to represent it.
- **Embedded Phonics**—children are taught letter-sound relationships in the context of reading.
- **Onset-Rime Instruction**—children identify the sound of the letter(s) before the onset (or first vowel) in a one-syllable word and the sound of the rime (or the remaining part of the word).

In this section of the book, you will find activities related to the above methods of phonics teaching. These activities will feature the following skills:

- word families
- consonants
- compound words
- "y" as a vowel
- contractions
- "-ing" endings
- diphthongs
- synonyms

- long vowels
- hard and soft "c"
- syllables
- consonant digraphs
- superlatives
- double vowels
- irregular double vowels
- antonyms

- short vowels
- hard and soft "g"
- blends
- "r"-controlled vowels
- suffixes
- vowel digraphs
- prefixes
- homonyms

Word Families Activities

Word Families

Standard: 5.5

Practice with word families is fun with this project.

Materials

- chalkboard and chalk
- yarn
- hole puncher
- construction paper (cut into 4" x 4" squares)
- markers
- word family cards (pages 25–26)
- chart paper
- clothes hanger
- copies of page 27

1. Explain to the students that many words have similar endings. These are called word families.
2. Write the following words on the chalkboard: *back, sack, pack, lack, track, smack.*
3. Draw students' attention to the *-ack* ending of each word. Explain that these words are in the *–ack* word family. Ask the students to think of other words in this word family (*rack, stack, tack*).
4. Write a list of other word families on chart paper (pages 25–26) and display them for the students.
5. Work together as a class to create words in selected word families.
6. Next have each child select three word families and write each word ending on a different construction-paper square.
7. The student then writes five words per word family, each on a different paper square.
8. Next, the student uses a hole puncher to punch a hole at the top and bottom of each card.
9. The student ties a length of yarn in each hole and then ties the cards together with the word-ending card at the top and the word cards below it. (The student will have a string of cards for each word family selected.)
10. Finally the student ties each string of words to a clothes hanger to make a mobile.
11. As a follow-up activity, have the students complete page 27.

Family Beach Ball

Standard: 5.5

Have students practice using word families with this lively game.

Materials

- word family cards (pages 25–26)
- beach ball
- scissors
- marker (optional)
- tape

1. Duplicate and cut apart the word family cards; then tape each card to a section of a beach ball. (You can also use a marker to write the words on the ball, if desired.)
2. To play, the students sit in a circle.
3. One student tosses the beach ball to another. The child who catches the ball looks at the card facing him or her.
4. Then the child adds a letter to the beginning of the word family card and says the word aloud.
5. Then the child tosses the ball to another. Play continues in this manner.

Family Beach Ball Cards

-ack	-ad
-ail	-all
-am	-ame
-an	-ap
-ash	-at
-ain	-ake
-ate	-aw
-ay	-eel

Family Beach Ball Cards *(cont.)*

-eep	-en
-ent	-est
-ice	-ill
-in	-ing
-og	-oil
-ood	-out
-own	-ug
-ump	-un

Word Family Fun

Complete each sentence with a word in the given word family.

1. The baseball player was up to _____.
-at

2. Don't go in the _____ without an umbrella.
-ain

3. What time did you _____ up this morning?
-ake

4. What did you _____?
-ay

5. I love the smell of the orange _____.
-eel

6. This toy is yours to _____.
-eep

7. My little sister learned to count to _____.
-en

8. Why did you _____ at me?
-ell

9. I went camping and slept in a _____.
-ent

10. Be sure to do your _____.
-est

11. Are you _____ waiting?
-ill

12. That's a beautiful gold _____.
-ing

Vowels and Consonants Activities

Vowel Review

Standard: 5.5

At the beginning of the school year, it may be necessary to spend a brief amount of time reviewing long- and short-vowel sounds. The following activity makes this review a fun experience.

Materials

- magazines
- scissors
- glue
- construction-paper cards (index card size)
- hole puncher
- yarn
- copies of pages 29–30

1. Begin the lesson by reviewing the long- and short- vowel sounds. Ask the students to think of words that represent each of the sounds.

2. Next, provide each student with magazines, scissors, glue, and 10 construction-paper cards.

3. Instruct each student to look for magazine pictures that represent one of the five short-vowel sounds and one of the five long-vowel sounds.

4. When a picture is found, the student cuts it out and glues it onto a card.

5. Have each student use a hole puncher to punch a hole at the top of each picture card.

6. Make a construction-paper label for each vowel sound and punch a hole at the bottom of each label.

7. Use lengths of yarn to attach the corresponding picture cards together as shown.

8. As a follow-up activity, have students complete pages 29–30.

Consonant Review

Standard: 5.5

Provide your students with a quick review of consonant sounds by completing page 31.

Materials

- copies of page 31
- pencils

1. Make copies of the Consonant Review on page 31.

2. Have students complete the page to review what they have learned about consonant sounds.

Short-Vowel Review

Complete each sentence below by writing a short-vowel word on the line. Use the Word Box to help you.

Word Box

truck	lock	ten	box	lunch
bed	gift	dig	went	cat
---

1. Close your eyes and count to _____.

2. What is inside the _____?

3. She _____ to school early today.

4. A big _____ is parked outside.

5. Did you buy the baby a _____ for her birthday?

6. Did you already eat _____?

7. My _____ is very soft.

8. My dog likes to _____ in the yard.

9. Don't forget to _____ the door.

10. Did you clean your room and make the _____ this morning?

   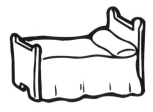

Read each word below. Write a new word on the line by changing the vowel to **a**, **e**, **i**, **o**, or **u**. (If possible, make more than one new word.)

1. tap _____

2. pet _____

3. mad _____

4. dug _____

5. trip _____

6. pot _____

Long-Vowel Review

Say the word at the beginning of each row. Circle the picture that has the same long-vowel sound.

1. deep			
2. cute			
3. fire			
4. flake			
5. joke			
6. tray			
7. tree			
8. boat			
9. fine			
10. make			

Consonant Review

Using the words in the Word Box, find words that have the given letter at the beginning, middle, or end. Write the words on the lines.

	Beginning	**Middle**	**End**
t	_____	_____	_____
l	_____	_____	_____
f	_____	_____	_____
m	_____	_____	_____
b	_____	_____	_____
p	_____	_____	_____
g	_____	_____	_____
n	_____	_____	_____

Word Box

bread	kitten	windy
carrot	smelly	fine
stuff	baffle	heaven
table	gentle	more
hammer	digger	tram
patch	hug	happy
leather	never	jeep
tell	dribble	cab

General Activities

The activities below correspond to reproducibles on pages 33–35.

Hard and Soft "c" and "g"

Standard: 5.5

Materials

- copies of pages 33–34
- scissors

1. Begin by focusing on the letter **c**.

2. Ask the children to tell the sounds **c** can make.

3. Review with them the concept of hard "c" and soft "c."

4. Do the same with the letter **g**.

5. Explain that there are a few simple rules that can help with identifying which sound the letters make.

✧ When **g** is followed by **a**, **i**, **o**, or **u**, it usually makes the **hard** sound.

✧ When **g** is followed by **e or y**, it usually makes the **soft** sound.

✧ When **c** is followed by **a**, **o**, or **u**, it usually makes the **hard** sound.

✧ When **c** is followed by **e**, **i**, or **y**, it usually makes the **soft** sound.

---

6. Instruct the students to keep these rules in mind as they complete the activity on page 33.

7. To assemble the game, duplicate the pages. Cut apart the word cards. Cut slits on the dotted lines on page 33.

8. To play, a student places the word cards in the slits below the corresponding headings.

Syllables

Standard: 5.5

Materials

- copies of page 35
- pencils

1. Review syllables with your students by having them identify the number of parts or beats in a word.

2. Explain that they can clap or tap the number of beats to determine the number of syllables.

3. Have the students continue syllable practice by completing page 35.

Hard and Soft "c" and "g"

Cut out the slits on the dotted lines. Place the word cards (page 34) below the correct headings.

Hard Sound

Soft Sound

Word Cards

gave	gel
give	giggle
goal	gobble
gush	guppy
gentle	gem
gym	gypsy
cabin	cent
cotton	cobbler
custard	cupboard
cellar	cement
citizen	city
cycle	cyclone

Count the Syllables

Put your phonics and phonemic awareness skills to the test. Say the name of each picture. Write the number of syllables you hear.

_____

_____

_____

_____

_____

_____

_____

_____

_____

_____

_____

_____

Compound Words Activity

Compound Words

Standard: 5.5

This activity will assist your students in learning or reviewing compound words.

Materials

- chart paper or chalkboard
- marker or chalk
- drawing paper
- crayons
- copies of pages 37–38

1. Explain to the students that a compound word is formed when two words are put together to make one word. For example, *rain + coat = raincoat*.

2. Ask the students to think of as many words as they can that combine two words.

3. Write their responses on chart paper or the chalkboard.

4. Ask individual students to approach the chart and use a marker to circle the two different parts of a word.

5. Distribute drawing paper to each student and instruct each one to make a word equation showing a compound word in pictures. For example, a student might draw a pea + a nut, which equals *peanut*.

6. Allow students to share and discuss their work.

7. Continue to practice using compound words with the activity on page 38.

8. Duplicate, laminate, and cut apart the cards on page 37.

9. Provide each student with a copy of the record sheet on page 38 and the cards from page 37.

10. The student uses the cards to make as many compound words as possible, and writes these words on the record sheet.

Word Cards

rain	coat	bow	space
ship	rocket	foot	ball
basket	base	sun	shine
bean	bag	tree	top
pea	nut	milk	man
pan	cake	snow	fall

Making Compound Words

How many compound words can you make? Use the word cards (page 37) to create as many compound words as you can. Write each word below.

Hint: Cards can be used more than once.

_____   _____

_____   _____

_____   _____

_____   _____

_____   _____

_____   _____

Rebus Words

Look at the pictures that represent each word part. Then write the compound word. An example has been done for you.

rain + drop   <u>raindrop</u>

1. up + hill   _____

2. nose + dive  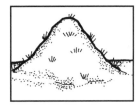 _____

3. star + fish  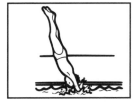 _____

4. light + house   _____

5. sail + boat 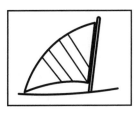  _____

General Activities *(cont.)*

The activities below correspond to the reproducibles on pages 41–49 and refer to Standard 5.5.

Blends

Materials

- copies of pages 41–44
- pencils

Many words contain blends. When two consonants are found together in a word and each letter makes its own sound, it is called a *blend*. For example, in the word *blend* the **b** and the **l** make their own sounds. Review different kinds of blends, such as *bl, gl, cl, fl, sl, st, sw, gr, br, tr,* etc. Be sure to discuss the fact that blends can also be found at the ends of words, as in *bunk* or *fast*. Practice using blends by having each student complete pages 41–44.

"y" as a Vowel

Materials

- copies of page 45
- pencils

Before distributing page 45, review the sounds that the letter **y** can make when used as a vowel— long "e" (*cherry*), long "i" (*try*), and short "i" (*gypsy*).

Consonant Digraphs

Discuss with the students the meaning of blends. Consonant diagraphs are a bit different. They are formed when two consonants together make one sound.

Materials

- chalkboard and chalk
- paper and pencils
- copies of pages 46–47

Provide examples, such as *th, sh,* or *kn*. Ask the students to tell the sound each consonant makes on its own and then point out the different sound that is made when the two letters are put together. Next, divide the students into small groups. Write the following digraphs on the chalkboard:

th	*ph*	*wr*	*ch*	*wh*	*sh*	*kn*

Instruct the groups to think of as many words as possible that contain these digraphs. Have each group write its words on a sheet of paper. Have students follow-up this activity by completing pages 46–47.

"r"-Controlled Vowels

Materials

- copies of pages 48–49

1. Duplicate, laminate, and cut apart the cards on pages 48–49. To play, two students deal the word cards. The "r"-controlled cards are placed in a stack facedown.

2. In turn, each child selects an "r" card. Then he or she determines whether or not the vowel plus r could be combined with a word card in his or her hand to make a word. For example, if the child picks the *ir* card, it could be combined with b___d to make the word *bird*.

3. If a word can be made, the child has a match and keeps both cards.

r Blends

Read each sentence. Fill in the blanks with the **r blends** that make sense.

Blends					
pr	**cr**	**dr**	**tr**	**fr**	**gr**

1. Kelly won first _____ ize.

2. Please answer the _____ ont door.

3. Mom asked me to _____ y the dishes.

4. How many _____ iends are coming to the party?

5. Do you like chocolate ice _____ eam?

6. Let me show you my magic _____ ick.

7. Last night I had the strangest _____ eam.

8. Didn't she do a _____ eat job?

9. Jesse thanked me for the birthday _____ esent.

10. Dad was running so he wouldn't miss the _____ ain.

11. The baby fell down and _____ ied.

12. I love mashed potatoes and _____ avy.

l Blends

Use the Word Box to find the *l blend* word that completes each sentence.

Word Box

play	blocks	plant	flute	blanket
flag	clock	sled	slipper	glass
planet	clown			
---

1. The _____ of the U.S.A. is red, white, and blue.

2. When will it be time to go outside to _____ ?

3. My little brother loves to build towers with _____ .

4. Will there be a _____ at your party?

5. My mom will _____ a garden on Saturday.

6. Mercury is the closest _____ to the sun.

7. The puppy chewed up my _____ .

8. Riding a _____ is scary, but fun.

9. Watch out for the broken _____ !

10. Can you read the time on that _____ ?

11. My favorite instrument is the _____ .

12. I like to curl up in a warm _____ .

"s" Blends

Use the **"s" blend** and the **word endings** to make as many words as possible. Write the words on the lines below. You may use the word parts more than once.

"s" Blends		
spr	sp	str
sm	sn	sw
sl	spl	sk
squ	sc	st

Word Endings			
-ail	-ate	-ore	-ed
-awk	-amp	-ar	-oop
-ent	-ing	-ill	-ump
-eam	-ash	-in	-el

_____ _____ _____

_____ _____ _____

_____ _____ _____

_____ _____ _____

_____ _____ _____

Final Blends

Use each ending blend to create a word. Challenge yourself and try to think of two words for each ending blend.

1. mp _____   _____

2. nd _____   _____

3. st _____   _____

4. sk _____   _____

5. nk _____   _____

6. ft _____   _____

7. nt _____   _____

8. lk _____   _____

9. lf _____   _____

Word Box

| hand | plant | stand | trunk | shelf | sink |

Write a word from the Word Box on each line to complete the sentences.

1. Mom stores blankets in the _____ by her bed.

2. I love to help my sister _____ a garden.

3. Please rinse the dishes in the _____ .

4. Why do you have a bandage on your _____ ?

5. I can't reach the book on the _____ .

6. Can you _____ on your head?

"y" as a Vowel

Sometimes the letter **y** is used as a vowel. It can make a long "i" sound, a short "i" sound, or a long "e" sound. Add a **y** to each word part and write the new word on the line. Beside each word write "short" or "long" to tell the sound it makes. The first one has been done for you.

	New Word	**Which Sound?**
1. sl _____	sly	long "i"
2. fr _____	_____	_____
3. famil _____	_____	_____
4. sill _____	_____	_____
5. sk _____	_____	_____
6. g _____ psy	_____	_____
7. c _____ cle	_____	_____
8. man _____	_____	_____
9. cherr _____	_____	_____
10. g _____ m	_____	_____

Think of three of your own words with "y" as a vowel. Write them on the lines below.

Long "i"	**Short "i"**	**Long "e"**
_____	_____	_____
_____	_____	_____
_____	_____	_____
_____	_____	_____
_____	_____	_____

Consonant Digraphs

When two consonants side-by-side make one sound, they are called a digraph. For example, **s** makes its own sound and so does **h**, but when they are put together they make a different sound (as in the words *brush* and *shape*).

Read the words below. Write each consonant diagraph on the line.

1. thirty   _____
2. phone   _____
3. write   _____
4. chew   _____
5. tough   _____
6. when   _____
7. shell   _____
8. knit   _____
9. kick   _____
10. sign   _____

Choose a word from the Word Box to complete each sentence.

Word Box

wrong	knife	mother	share	wheel	chalk

1. Which woman is your _____ ?

2. Is that _____ sharp?

3. The teacher had _____ on her hands.

4. What's _____ with you?

5. I need to fix the _____ on my bike.

6. Would you like to _____ my candy bar?

Where's the Digraph?

Consonant digraphs are found at the beginning, in the middle, and at the end of words. Using the Word Box, decide where each digraph is located and write the word in the correct column.

Word Box

benches	ship	write	orphan	they	know
rough	why	gnaw	chirp	graph	telephone
much	brush	brother	other	tickle	birthday
earth	sick	tough			

Beginning **Middle** **End**

Word Cards

h _____ n	h _____ t
f _____	ch _____ ch
_____ ange	b _____ d
c _____ k	tw _____ l
f _____ m	g _____ l
p _____ k	sk _____ t
sp _____ k	tig _____
sh _____ p	bett _____
b _____ n	nev _____
h _____ ry	matt _____

"r" Cards

ar	er
ir	or
ur	ar
er	ir
or	ur
ar	er
ir	or
ur	ar
er	ir
or	ur

General Activities *(cont.)*

The activities below correspond to the reproducibles on pages 51–57 and refer to Standard 5.5.

Contractions

Materials

- copies of pages 51–52
- pencils

A *compound word* is made when two words are put together to make one word. Contractions combine two words as well, except that one or both of the words are shortened. When *I am* becomes *I'm*, the **a** in *am* is replaced by an apostrophe. Have the students complete pages 51–52.

Superlatives

Materials

- copies of page 53
- pencils

Superlatives are words that compare, such as *big, bigger, biggest* or *tall, taller, tallest*. Help your students understand this concept by making statements and guiding them in making comparisons. For example, "Billy is a young boy, but Billy has a baby brother. We would say that Billy's brother is . . . than he is." Continue in this manner using words, such as *small, tiny, cute, smart*, etc. Complete page 53 for further practice.

Suffixes

Materials

- copies of page 54
- pencils

Many words have prefixes and suffixes that contribute to their meanings. For example, the prefix un- means opposite. The opposite of *do* is *undo*. The prefix pre- means before, so a *pretest* is a test that comes before another test. By reviewing the meanings of prefixes and suffixes with your students, you are providing them with skills that will help them determine the meanings of some new words they encounter. See the list below for prefixes, suffixes, and their meanings. Have students complete page 54 for additional practice.

un—opposite	pre—before	dis—don't
ness—a state of being	ful—having a lot of	less—having little of

"-ing" Endings

Materials

- copies of pages 55–57
- brass fastener
- paper clip
- game markers

To assemble the game, cut out the spinner. Press a brass fastener through the dot in the center. Attach a large paper clip to the fastener. To play the game, a child places his or her marker on START. He or she then spins the spinner and reads the rule. Then the child looks for the first space on the game trail containing a word that would use this rule for adding "-ing." The child moves his or her game piece to that space. Play continues until a player reaches FINISH. Complete page 55 for further practice.

Contractions

When two words are put together to form one word, it is called a *contraction*.

> **For example:** *I am* becomes *I'm*. *We are* becomes *we're.*

Notice that some of the letters are left out and they are replaced with an apostrophe.

Look at the contractions below. Write the two words that were combined. Then write the letters that were replaced with an apostrophe. The first one has been done for you.

Contractions	Two Words	Replaced Letter(s)
1. I'm	I am	a
2. isn't		
3. you're		
4. don't		
5. let's		
6. it's		
7. we'll		
8. I've		
9. wasn't		
10. aren't		

Forming Contractions

Use the list below to assist you in making contractions.

not = n't	is = 's	will = 'll
us = 's	are = 're	have = 've

Remember that *will not* doesn't follow the rules. *Will not* becomes *won't.*

Combine each pair of words below to make a contraction.

1. we are   _____

2. are not   _____

3. they will   _____

4. it will   _____

5. could not   _____

6. you are   _____

7. he is   _____

8. do not   _____

9. can not   _____

10. I have   _____

11. she will   _____

12. was not   _____

Superlatives

Some word endings help us to compare objects. The "-er" ending means even more. See the example below. One box is small. A smaller box is even more small. The "-est" ending means the most. The smallest box is the most small.

> For example:
>   The box is small.
>   That box is smaller.
>   This box is the smallest.

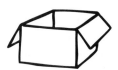

Add "-er" or "-est" to the word below the line to complete each sentence.

1. Mike is _____ than his dad.
      tall

2. Amy is _____ than her mom.
      short

3. Kelly is the _____ in her family.
      young

4. That present is in the _____ box.
      big

5. The black puppy is _____ than the white one.
      fat

6. Who is the _____ in your family?
      old

7. This hallway is _____ than that one.
      wide

8. That is the _____ car I have ever seen.
      small

Write a sentence for each word below.

cute _____

cuter _____

cutest _____

Suffixes

A suffix can be used to change the meaning of a word.

> For example: Can I *help* you?
> I feel *helpless.*

Change each base word below by adding a different suffix. (Put an X in the box if the base word and suffix don't make a real word.) The first two have been done for you.

Base Word	"–ful"	"–less"	"–ness"	"–ly"
hope	hopeful	hopeless	X	X
kind	X	X	kindness	kindly
1. faith				
2. ill				
3. sad				
4. color				
5. slow				
6. sick				
7. help				
8. thank				
9. neat				
10. loud				
11. care				
12. pain				

"-ing" and "-ed" Endings

Follow the rules to add "-ed" and "-ing" to the words below.

Rule #1:

When a short-vowel word ends in a single consonant, double the consonant and add "-ed" or "-ing."

	"-ed"	"-ing"
1. skip	_____	_____
2. hop	_____	_____
3. bat	_____	_____
4. beg	_____	_____
5. drip	_____	_____
6. stop	_____	_____

Rule #2:

When a word ends in silent "e," drop the "e" and add "-ed" or "-ing."

	"-ed"	"-ing"
1. smile	_____	_____
2. bake	_____	_____
3. file	_____	_____
4. vote	_____	_____
5. tune	_____	_____
6. name	_____	_____

"-ing" Endings Game

Directions:

1. Place a game piece on START.
2. Spin the spinner (see page 57). Read the rule for adding "-ing."
3. Find the first word that would use that rule for adding "-ing."
4. Move your game piece to that space.

START	map	tan	make
			run
track	jump	help	yell
trip			
rain	sway	skip	feel
			come
FINISH	change	fill	bike

Spinner

When a short-vowel word ends with a single consonant, double the consonant and add "-ing."

When a word ends in silent "e," drop the "e" and add "-ing."

When a word ends with two consonants, just add "-ing."

When a long-vowel word ends in a single consonant, just add "-ing."

General Activities *(cont.)*

Double Vowels

Standard: 5.5

Pages 59–60 will assist your students in identifying the sounds made by double vowel combinations, such as *oa, ea, ai, ie, ue*.

Materials

- copies of pages 59–60
- pencils

Before distributing these pages to your students, be sure to review the sounds with them and have them think of words that contain these letter combinations.

Vowel Digraphs

Standard: 5.5

Materials

- copies of page 61
- pencils

Reading words with vowel digraphs can be tricky because they don't make the sounds typically associated with the letters. See the list of digraphs and words below. Review these with your students. Then distribute page 61 for student practice.

> *oo* as in *book* or *moon*　　　*ea* as in *bread*　　　*au* as in *August*
> *ei* as in *eight*　　　*aw* as in *lawn*

Diphthongs

Standard: 5.5

Materials

- copies of page 62
- pencils

Explain to your students that a *diphthong* is made when two vowels blend together to make one sound. Display a list of diphthongs (see below) and ask the students to think of other words that contain these sounds. Have students complete page 62 for further practice using diphthongs.

oy Words	*oi* Words	*ow* Words	*ou* Words	*ew* Words
toy	soil	owl	ground	dew
joy	join	how	round	few
soy	foil	town	house	grew

Double-Vowel Passages

Underline each double-vowel word in the passages below. Write each double-vowel word on a line and then write the sound it makes. The first one has been done for you.

The Green Leaf

One day a seal was swimming in the sea when he saw a leaf floating by. "My, my," said the seal. "That leaf is far from home. Why, it is as green as a leaf can be. I wonder if it blew off the deck of a boat." He picked it up and took it to the shore. "It would be a shame for the leaf to stay soaked." The seal placed the leaf on land. "There you go, leaf. Now you're clean and dry."

Double-Vowel Word		**Sound**	
seal		long "e"	
word	vowel	word	vowel
_____	_____	_____	_____
_____	_____	_____	_____
_____	_____	_____	_____
_____	_____	_____	_____
_____	_____	_____	_____
_____	_____	_____	_____

Toad on the Road

A happy toad hopped cheerfully down the road. "What a glorious day it is," he exclaimed. "The leaves are changing to beautiful shades of yellow and orange. I do believe that fall is the best season of all." Toad took a seat and gazed at the sky. There was a slight chill in the air, but he didn't mind. He just relaxed, ate his midday meal, and then continued down the road.

Double-Vowel Word		**Sound**	
toad		long "o"	
word	vowel	word	vowel
_____	_____	_____	_____
_____	_____	_____	_____
_____	_____	_____	_____
_____	_____	_____	_____
_____	_____	_____	_____

Double Vowels

Circle the words in each row that have the given sound. The first one has been done for you.

1. Long "e"	(seat)	(meat)	tried
2. Long "o"	seek	soap	boat
3. Long "a"	rain	ran	pail
4. Long "i"	tie	twist	lie
5. Long "u"	blue	glue	tub
6. Long "e"	bet	bean	jeep
7. Long "o"	outer	coat	float
8. Long "a"	mail	apple	claim
9. Long "i"	tried	mixed	cried
10. Long "a"	tail	beak	bait
11. Long "e"	sell	team	heat
12. Long "i"	fried	tried	seat

Write a sentence using each of the sounds to make double-vowel words.

Long "a": _____

Long "e": _____

Long "i": _____

Long "o": _____

Long "u": _____

Vowel Digraphs

Circle the double "o" word in each sentence. Decide if the word sounds like *book* or *soon*. Write that word on the line.

1. Are you ready for school? _____

2. Did you get one scoop or two? _____

3. She is a good dog. _____

4. The air feels cool. _____

5. Is it almost noon? _____

6. There is so much soot in the fireplace. _____

7. Let me take a look. _____

8. Did you help your mother cook dinner? _____

9. My house is at the end of the loop. _____

10. Don't let my brother fool you. _____

11. Is that the photograph you took? _____

12. A dictionary is a useful tool. _____

Diphthongs

A *diphthong* is made when two vowels blend together to make one sound.

For example:

oy in *boy*   ou in *round*   oi in *foil*   ew in *few*   ow in *down*

Complete each sentence below using a word from the Word Box.

Word Box

toy	enjoy	boy	out	house
found	oil	coins	boil	down
owl	how	few	blew	drew

1. I hope you will _____ your present.

2. Is that the picture you _____ ?

3. I bought a new _____ at the store.

4. The wind _____ my hat off.

5. James is a nice little _____ .

6. How many _____ are in your pocket?

7. Did you let the dog _____ ?

8. My mom taught me _____ to paint.

9. My _____ is blue and white:

10. My jacket was in the lost and _____ box.

11. Can I have a _____ pieces of candy?

12. Dad and I saw an _____ in the tree.

13. The _____ made the road slippery.

14. Krissi's cat won't come _____ from the roof.

15. It takes a while for water to _____ .

General Activities *(cont.)*

Prefixes

Standard: 5.5

Materials

- paper and pencils
- copies of page 64

1. Write the following words on the chalkboard:

    clear　　　　　　*read*　　　　　　*like*

2. Ask students to define each word. Then add a prefix to each word.

    unclear　　　　*reread*　　　　*dislike*

3. Ask the students to compare the base words to the words with prefixes and explain how the words changed when the prefixes were added.

4. Distribute dictionaries to pairs of students and ask them to find words in the dictionary that begin with the "un-" prefix. Instruct each pair to make a list of all the words it finds where "un-" is used as a prefix.

5. Then have each pair of students define the words on the list.

6. For more practice with prefixes, have students complete page 64.

Synonym and Antonyms

Standard: 5.8

Materials

- copies of pages 65–66

Duplicate pages 65–66. Laminate and cut apart the puzzle pieces. Explain to the students that *synonyms* are words that have the same or almost the same meaning, such as *smile/grin*. *Antonyms* are words that have opposite meanings, such as *good/bad*. Show the students that the puzzle pieces will fit together when the synonyms and the antonyms are matched.

Homophones

Standard: 5.8

Materials

- chalkboard and chalk
- copies of page 67
- pencils

Write the words below on the chalkboard.

maid/made	weak/week	one/won	eight/eight	bee/be	sail/sale
knows/nose	weight/wait	I/eye	die/dye	see/sea	

Draw students' attention to the fact that each set of words is pronounced the same, but spelled differently. The meanings are also different. These are homophones. Have students practice using homophones by completing page 67.

Prefixes

When a word part is added to the beginning of a base word, it can change its meaning. For example, when "dis-" is added to *like*, the word *dislike* is formed. This word means *not like*. See the definitions of "dis-", "un-", and "re-" below.

> **"dis-"** means *not—disapprove* means *to not approve*
>
> **"un-"** means *not—unable* means *not able*
>
> **"re-"** means *do again—retell* means *to tell again*

Define each word below.

1. unfair _____
2. disagree _____
3. reread _____
4. disfavor _____
5. untrue _____
6. rewrap _____
7. uncertain _____
8. disable _____
9. disobey _____
10. reload _____
11. dislike _____
12. unsure _____
13. uneven _____
14. redo _____

Add "un-", "re-", or "dis-" to the words below to make real words.

1. happy _____
2. made _____
3. honest _____
4. caring _____
5. build _____
6. opened _____
7. fill _____

Synonym Puzzles

upset	story	quiet
angry	tale	shy
listen	say	unhappy
hear	tell	sad
store	large	injure
shop	big	hurt

Antonym Puzzles

strong	hard	come
weak	easy	go
sick	above	lost
healthy	below	found
friend	inside	happy
enemy	outside	sad

Homophones

When two words sound the same, but have different meanings and spellings, they are called *homophones*. For example, *maid* and *made* are homophones. A *maid* is a person who cleans and *made* means created.

Look at the Word Box below. Decide which word completes each sentence and write it on the line.

Word Box

our/hour   one/won   bee/be

I/eye   right/write

1. My sister turned _____ year old.

2. I can hear the buzzing _____ .

3. Who _____ the game?

4. Please _____ your name on your paper.

5. I'll come over in an _____ .

6. Did _____ dog run through your yard?

7. Raise your _____ hand.

8. I have something in my _____ .

9. Kelly and _____ are friends.

10. Where will you _____ after school today?

Assessment Chart

Student Name:		
Phonics Skill	**Date Introduced**	**Date of Mastery**
short vowels		
long vowels		
consonants		
hard and soft "c"		
hard and soft "g"		
syllables		
compound words		
blends		
"y" as a vowel		
consonant digraphs		
"r"-controlled vowels		
contractions		
superlatives		
suffixes		
"-ing" endings		
double vowels		
vowel digraphs		
diphthongs		
prefixes		
synonyms		
antonyms		
homophones		

Fluency

Fluency refers to a child's ability to read quickly with minimal errors.

Fluent readers have the ability to:

- recognize words with automaticity
- group words into meaningful chunks
- connect ideas in print to prior knowledge

- draw meaning from print
- read with little effort
- read with expression

Less fluent readers:

- read slowly
- read choppily (or word by word)
- take great effort to read

- focus on decoding
- pay little attention to meaning

When speaking of fluency, you will likely encounter the word *automaticity*. This word is often used interchangeably with fluency, which is not entirely accurate.

Automaticity refers to reading that is quick, effortless, and automatic. Fluency involves automaticity, but also refers to reading with expression. A child who reads with fluency reads with automaticity, but a child who reads with automaticity is not necessarily considered a fluent reader.

Why Is Fluency Important?

Fluency helps children to move from decoding and word recognition to comprehension. There is a strong correlation between fluency and comprehension, which is why instruction in this area is so important. The reading skills of fluent readers are largely automatic, which allows children to interpret meaning rather than focus on deciphering letter sounds and individual words. They are essentially able to see words and automatically comprehend their meanings. Fluency becomes an area of focus after a child learns to break the code, making it an important focus for third grade students.

Educators tend to teach fluency in two different ways:

- **Repeated and Monitored Oral Reading**—this method of fluency instruction involves guidance from a teacher while a child reads a passage aloud several times.
- **Independent Silent Reading**—this method involves many opportunities for students to read silently on their own.

It is believed that repeated and monitored oral reading is the most effective way to assist children with fluency development. This is not the case, however, for the traditional "round-robin" reading where children take turns reading aloud. Aside from the anxiety that round-robin reading can bring about with some children, it also only involves the one-time reading of small portions of text. Proper fluency instruction involves the repeated reading of relatively simple passages and the modeling of reading (pauses and expression) by more proficient readers.

This section of the book provides activities in the following areas:

- general fluency activities
- choral reading
- partner reading

- student-adult reading
- tape-assisted reading

- assessment
- Readers Theater

General Activities

Keep on Reading

Standards: 5.1, 5.9, and 5.10

Materials

- reading materials

✧ Reading aloud to children never ceases to be an important activity. In fact, your students will learn to read with better fluency if they hear others reading smoothly, accurately, and with expression. Use the following tips to guide your daily read-aloud time.

✧ Read aloud to your students for at least 30 minutes a day.

✧ Select chapter books to read so the students will have ongoing interest in longer stories.

✧ Try to select books with interesting characters.

✧ Use expression that matches each character's personality.

✧ Engage the students in the story by periodically asking questions about the story. Be sure not to go overboard with questioning, as the students should be allowed to enjoy the fluent reading of the story.

Again and Again

Standards: 5.1, 5.9, and 5.10

When students are given the opportunity to read passages several times, they increase their fluency. Fluency improves even more when students listen to fluent readers and then repeat the same passages. Remember that when working on fluency, students should be reading passages at or slightly below their reading levels.

Materials

- short passages at appropriate reading levels for students

1. Begin by explaining to the students that reading smoothly is an important skill.

2. Select a passage of text to read aloud to the students. Read in a choppy manner, pausing between words.

3. Ask the students to respond to the way you read the passage. Was it easy to understand? Was it enjoyable to listen to?

4. Tell the students that they will have the opportunity to listen to you read and then repeat the reading to practice fluency.

5. Begin by allowing the students to look through the passage and read it silently.

6. Then read aloud the first two sentences and have the students read it aloud afterward. Continue in this manner through the entire passage of text.

7. Draw students' attention to the way they are able to read smoothly when copying you.

General Activities *(cont.)*

Developing Character
Standards: 5.1, 5.9, and 5.10

Part of fluency involves reading with expression. Good readers use expression when reading any text aloud. They also change their expression when reading the words of a particular character. This activity will help your students learn to read with expression.

Material
- children's book (such as *Bunnicula* by Deborah and James Howe)

1. Explain to the students that this is a story that is told by the family sheepdog.
2. Ask the students to think about how a sheepdog might sound if it was able to speak our language.
3. Tell the students that there are other characters in the story who speak, such as the family and the family's cat.
4. Begin reading the story, drawing attention to the different characters. Be sure to vary your voice from character to character to model the use of expression.
5. Encourage the students to borrow the book from you during free time to practice reading parts of the story using expression.

Easing Anxiety
Standard: 5.1
Materials
- reading passages

Be sure to allow your students to practice the reading of a passage before reading it aloud. This helps to alleviate some of the anxiety of reading aloud and helps to improve fluency. Most of us know the feeling of having to read "on the spot." By allowing each student the chance to familiarize himself or herself with the passage and focusing on reading smoothly and with expression, you'll notice that the students are more likely to relax and even listen to their peers read once the anxiety is relieved.

Parent Involvement
Standards: 5.1, 5.9, and 5.10

Getting parents involved in the practice of reading skills is a great way to help students improve their reading skills. Many parents need tips that provide ideas for working with their children in reading.

Reading can be made enjoyable in many ways, including:
- reading aloud
- taking turns reading passages
- being an expressive reader
- allowing a child to practice before reading aloud

Materials
- copies of page 72

Duplicate the Parent Letter on page 72 and send it home to parents to provide them with more detailed ways to read to and with their children.

Parent Letter

Dear Parent,

We are working on the improvement of reading fluency. *Fluency* refers to the ability to read smoothly, quickly, accurately, and with expression. You can assist your child with fluency at home in several ways.

1. **Read, read, read.** Even in the upper grades, it is important for you to read aloud to your child. It's good for your child to read to you, but it is still very important for him or her to hear examples of good reading. So head to the library, pick out a great book, and enjoy reading aloud to your child.

2. **Take turns.** When reading aloud with your child, take turns reading the text. You can alternate reading different sentences and paragraphs, or you can read a sentence and have your child repeat you by reading the same sentence. Allowing your child to copy the way you read will assist in the improvement of fluency.

3. **Be expressive.** Model for your child how to read with expression. Your child is learning to read basic text with expression, as well as using different expression when characters in the story have dialog. As your child improves expression, you'll notice reading that is smooth and pleasing to the ear.

4. **Encourage practice.** The purpose of fluency practice is to increase the manner in which the child reads. In order to do this effectively, it is necessary to allow your child to rehearse the reading of a book or passage. By doing this, he or she will be able to focus on speed, accuracy, and expression, rather than on figuring out unfamiliar words.

Your participation with fluency development is greatly appreciated. Happy reading!

Sincerely,

_____

teacher's signature

General Activities *(cont.)*

Guest Readers

Standards: 5.1, 5.9, and 5.10

Students usually have the opportunity to hear a few people read to them, such as teachers, librarians, and family members, but it is important for them to hear other people read as well. To provide this opportunity on a regular basis, make the role of guest reader one of your parent helper jobs. These experiences will demonstrate to your students that many people value and enjoy reading.

Materials

- copies of invitation (page 74)

1. Ask interested parents to visit the classroom on a particular day and time.
2. You can provide the books for the parent or have him or her select a few favorites.
3. You might also want to invite other people to be guest readers, such as the principal, the P.E. teacher, the art teacher, a custodian, etc.
4. Duplicate the letter on page 74 as an invitation for your guest readers.

Reading Level

Standards: 5.10, 5.12

Materials

- short passages at appropriate reading levels for students

When working on fluency development, it is important to select text that is at students' independent reading levels. You will need to designate different passages for students to ensure that they are working with text that is at the appropriate level. The National Reading Panel (2001) suggests the following for determining reading levels:

- **Independent Level**—this refers to easy text that contains only 1 in 20 difficult words for the student. The student should have a 95% success rate.

- **Instructional Level**—this text is more challenging, but not too difficult. The student should only encounter 1 in 10 difficult words with a 90% success rate.

- **Frustration Level**—this level refers to text that is very challenging for the child, with more than 1 in 10 difficult words. The student would have a less than 90% rate of success.

Guest Reader Invitation

WANTED:

GUEST READERS

◈ Do you like to read aloud?

◈ Do you enjoy reading children's books?

◈ Do you like to make children smile?

If so, we invite you to volunteer in _____'s class as a guest reader.

As a guest reader, you will:

- bring a few favorite children's books to class.
- sit with a group of children and read the books aloud.
- receive the satisfaction of bringing the joy of reading to children.

Please indicate below when you would like to visit our class.

_____

_____

We look forward to your visit and listening to our new Guest Reader.

Sincerely,

_____
teacher's signature

General Activities *(cont.)*

Quiet, Please

Standards: 5.9, 5.10

Provide your students with a quiet place in the classroom to practice reading aloud.

Materials

- copy of Quiet Corner Expectations (page 76)
- bookcases, file cabinets, rolling chalkboards or whiteboards
- pillows, beanbags, or carpet squares
- lamp or other light source
- construction paper
- marker

1. Use moveable furniture to create a peaceful area that is separated from the rest of the classroom.
2. Add comfort to this area by providing pillows, beanbags, or carpet squares.
3. Be sure there is adequate lighting in this area and, if necessary, provide a lamp.
4. Copy the list on page 76 onto construction paper. Post the list and include the number of students to use the area at one time.
5. Also post a schedule of students designated to use the area on particular days.

New Word Review

Standard: 5.8

You can assist your students with fluency by reviewing the meaning and pronunciation of new words that will be encountered in text.

Materials

- reading passage
- index cards
- marker
- resealable plastic bags

1. Review a reading passage and identify words that may be unfamiliar to your students.
2. Write each new word on a different index card. Prepare a set of word cards for each student in the group.
3. Provide each student with a set of cards and review the words one by one.
4. Assist your students with pronouncing each word as well as discussing its meaning.
5. As a follow-up activity, put sets of word cards in resealable plastic bags and place them at a learning center. Encourage the students to review the words in their free time.
6. Also, provide a copy of the reading passage containing the words and encourage the students to practice reading the text.
7. Remember that the goal of fluency practice is to focus on smooth reading and expression, rather than on decoding text or deciphering meaning.

Quiet Corner Expectations

✧ Only two students may use the area at one time.

✧ Come to the quiet corner with a book that is easy to read.

✧ Spend your time in the quiet corner reading aloud quietly.

✧ Pay attention to your reading accuracy, rate, and expression.

General Activities *(cont.)*

Get Ready to Read

Standard: 5.1

To ensure that fluency practice will be productive, encourage your students to read text passages before they come to reading group time.

Material

- reading passage that will be featured during group time

1. Be sure that students know what text will be used during group reading time.

2. Allow students time to review this text ahead of time. Encourage them to focus on reading with accuracy and expression, and seek assistance with reading unknown words.

3. Explain to the students that by practicing the passage before coming to reading group, they will have an easier time reading smoothly and also paying attention to the meaning of the passage.

Fluency Demonstration

Standards: 5.1, 5.9, and 5.10

Draw students' attention to the elements of fluent reading.

Materials

- reading materials (such as big books and poetry)

1. Demonstrate the difference between choppy reading and smooth reading.

2. Ask the students which form of reading is more pleasing to the ear.

3. Show the students how to pause when a comma is encountered.

4. Demonstrate the difference between reading in a monotone voice and reading with expression.

5. Draw attention to the tone of your voice as you read.

6. Demonstrate the way the voice can change to match the personality of a character when reading dialog.

7. Be sure to make reading materials available, such as big books and poetry, so children can practice reading independently or with partners during free time.

Repeated Reading Activity

Repeated Reading

Standards: 5.9, 5.10, and 5.12

Encourage your students to practice reading fluency independently.

Materials

- copies of page 79 (completed)
- access to texts at the appropriate reading level
- fluency practice instructions (below)
- copies of fluency graph (page 80)
- two-pocket folder
- stop watch or clock with a second hand
- colored pencils or markers

1. Duplicate a copy of page 79 for each student.
2. Complete the chart for each child with the reading passages, books, poems, etc. that the child should use for reading fluency practice.
3. Duplicate a copy of the instructions below and the Fluency Graph (page 80) for each child.
4. Place the reading chart, fluency practice instructions, and fluency graph in a folder for the child.
5. Explain to the students that when they practice reading, they should pay attention to how smoothly they are reading, read at a comfortable speed, and use expression.
6. Demonstrate to the students how to complete the fluency graph after their timed reading.
7. At designated times, the child reviews fluency practice instructions and then practices reading the texts you have selected.

Fluency Practice Instructions

✧ Select a passage of text from the chart completed by your teacher.
✧ Read the text by yourself.
✧ Ask for help with pronouncing unfamiliar words.
✧ Ask a classmate to read the text with you.
✧ Take turns reading the text with a classmate.
✧ Be sure to pay attention to your partner's fluency and your own.
✧ Read the passage by yourself as fast as you can.
✧ Ask a classmate to time your reading for 30 seconds.
✧ Record your results on the fluency graph.

Approved Reading Selections

Name: _____

Teacher: Complete this chart with a list of books, passages, poetry selections, etc., that are at the child's independent reading level.

Student: After practicing a selection, make a check mark in the box beside it.

Name of Selection	Completed

Fluency Graph

Name: _____

Record the date of your timed reading. Then color the bar on the graph that most closely matches the number of words read in 30 seconds.

Number of Words Read (30 seconds)

130				
120				
110				
100				
90				
80				
70				
60				
50				
40				
30				
20				
10				

Date _____   Date _____   Date _____   Date _____

Student-Adult Reading Activity

Recording the Facts

Standards: 5.9, 5.10

Motivate your students to read aloud and focus on fluency by allowing them to have read-aloud time with you, an instructional assistant, or another adult.

Materials

- reading passage (appropriate reading level)
- copies of the guide below
- copies of Fluency Chart Instructions (page 82)
- copies of chart (page 83)

Work with the student in the following way:

1. The student reads for a designated period of time. (This should be a short interval, such as one minute.)

2. The adult completes the chart on page 83 by recording the student's name and fluency progress.

3. Page 82 provides details to assist in the completion of the chart.

4. The list below can be provided to an instructional assistant or another classroom helper to guide this student-adult reading time.

Guide to Fluency Practice

✧ Be sure the child has selected a book at his or her reading level.

✧ There should be no more than 1 in 20 difficult words.

✧ Ask the child to read a passage to you. (Pay attention to the child's reading rate, fluency, and expression.)

✧ Assist the child in reading smoothly by modeling the reading of a sentence and then asking the child to repeat it.

✧ Try reading the passage together. Read at a comfortable rate and be sure to add expression.

✧ For more fluent readers, focus on the use of expression and a pleasing tone of voice.

Fluency Chart Instructions

Use the information below to assist you in completing the fluency chart on page 83.

Passage—Record the passage that the child read (book, magazine, or text).

Fluency—Record the child's ability to read smoothly, quickly, accurately, and with expression. Comment on the child's fluency according to the descriptions below.

Smooth Reading: Listen as the child reads the passage. Pay attention to the manner in which the child reads.

- Does he or she hesitate between words?
- Does the reading sound "choppy"?
- Does the child have a consistent pace when reading?

Reading Rate: The goal of fluency is not to read as quickly as possible, but rather to read at a comfortable pace.

- Does the child read at a rate that is pleasant to listen to and easy to comprehend?

Accuracy: As the child reads, pay attention to the number of mistakes made. The child would receive a positive comment if he or she is able to read with 80–90% accuracy.

Expression: Part of reading fluently involves the ability to read with expression. This might involve varying the tone of voice when reading. This also involves varying the voice when different characters speak. Consider the following questions:

- Does the child read in a monotone voice?
- Does the child vary his or her tone of voice?
- Does the child vary his or her voice when reading dialog?

Child's Comments: This portion of the chart is important to complete because it encourages self-evaluation. After the child reads the passage, ask him or her the questions below and record pertinent responses.

- How do your feel about the way you read the passage?
- Was the passage difficult for you?
- Was your reading choppy or smooth?
- Did you read slowly or at a quick pace?
- Did you make many mistakes?
- How do you feel about your use of expression?

Fluency Chart

Name/ Date	Passage	Fluency				
		Smooth Reading	Reading Rates	Accuracy	Expression	Child's Comments

Choral Reading Activities

Big Book Read-Alouds

Standards: 5.9, 5.10

Big books are not only an excellent tool for modeling reading, they are also useful for choral reading. The large print in these books makes it possible for a group of children to see and read the text.

Materials

- big book
- easel or chalkboard tray
- pointer (optional)

1. To engage your students in the choral reading of a big book, display the book on an easel or the chalk tray of the chalkboard.

2. Use a pointer or your finger to point to the words as the children read them aloud together.

3. Assist the children in establishing a rhythm to their group reading. Draw students' attention to places where pauses are appropriate and emphasize the use of expression.

4. Periodically, you may want to model the reading of a page and then ask the students to copy your rate and expression by choral reading the page again.

Making Comparisons

Standard: 5.9

Have your students read different kinds of books to compare reading tone, expression, etc.

Materials

- variety of books that have different patterns and rhythms, such as:

> Kellogg, Steven. *Can I Keep Him?* Puffin, 1992.
>
> Munsch, Robert. *Pigs.* Annick Press, 1992.
>
> Numeroff, Laura Joffe. *If You Give a Mouse a Cookie.* Laura Geringer, 1985.
>
> Sharmat, Marjorie Weinman. *Gila Monsters Meet You at the Airport.* Scott Foresman, 1990.
>
> Van Allsburg, Chris. *Jumanji.* Houghton Mifflin Co., 1981.

1. Select a few books to read aloud to your students.

2. Ask them to listen to the difference in the rhythm of the words overall mood and tone of the story.

3. For example, *Pigs* by Robert Munsch is a story with silly, upbeat events. *Gila Monsters Meet You at the Airport* by Marjorie Weinman Sharmat contains dialog by a character who complains about moving to a new location.

4. Read different books with various tones, moods, and rhythm in your voice.

5. Explain that different kinds of stories call for different kinds of expression.

6. Have the children practice reading with different rhythms and tones by repeating sentences in different stories.

Tape-Assisted Reading Activities

Record-Listen-Record

Standards: 5.1, 5.9, 5.10, and 5.12

Help your students increase their fluency with the following activity.

Materials

- reading passage at independent reading level
- tape recorder with microphone and headphones
- audio tape

1. Instruct a student to practice reading a text passage that is at his or her independent reading level.
2. After practicing, the student records his or her reading of the passage.
3. Then the student listens to the recording through headphones while following along with the passage.
4. Encourage the student to pay attention to his or her reading rate, accuracy, and smoothness of reading.
5. After reviewing the recording, the student records the passage again to try to make improvements.

Audio Books

Standards: 5.1, 5.9, and 5.10

Many children's books are available on cassette tape or CD. These books are often accompanied by the printed forms of the books. You can even record your own books for students.

Materials

- audio recording of a children's book
- printed form of the book
- tape recorder or CD player
- headphones

1. Set up a listening center with a tape recorder and headphones.
2. At the center, a child plays the tape and follows along in the book as the narrator reads.
3. Remind the child to pay attention to the smooth way in which the narrator reads and the expression in the narrator's voice.
4. Provide different kinds of books for the children to enjoy on tape. The more examples of smooth, accurate reading a child experiences, the better he or she will learn to read fluently.

Tape-Assisted Reading Activities *(cont.)*

Follow the Narrator

Standards: 5.1, 5.9, and 5.10

This activity will provide fluency modeling for your students.

Materials

- audio recording of a children's book
- printed form of the book
- tape recorder
- headphones

1. Similar to the activity on page 85, set up a listening center with a tape recorder, headphones, and a book on tape (including a printed copy of the book).

2. While the narrator reads the story, have the child follow along by pointing to the words as the narrator reads them.

3. After listening to the story once, instruct the child to listen to it on another occasion.

4. This time the child reads along with the narrator, attempting to follow the narrator's reading rate, pauses, and expression.

Your Voice on Tape

Standards: 5.1, 5.9, and 5.10

Encourage your students to take responsibility for their fluency development with this activity.

Materials

- tape recorder
- microphone
- children's book or reading passage
- copies of page 87

1. Provide a tape recorder and a microphone at a learning center. (This learning center should be situated in a relatively quiet area of the classroom.)

2. Instruct a child to select a reading passage at an appropriate reading level. The student should practice reading the passage several times.

3. Then the child records himself or herself reading the passage.

4. Finally, have the child listen to the tape recording. Ask the child to evaluate his or her reading and determine areas of improvement.

5. Duplicate and distribute copies of page 87 to guide the students as they evaluate their fluency.

Fluency Evaluation

Student Directions: Practice reading a passage. Ask for help with reading any words that are unfamiliar to you. Record your voice as you read the passage. Complete the top part of this page to evaluate your reading fluency.

Name: _____

Date: _____

Name of passage: _____

My reading was:	very smooth	somewhat smooth	choppy
My reading rate was:	too fast	too slow	just right

I made mistakes reading these words:

_____

_____

Did I use expression?   Yes   No

Here is my plan for improvement:

_____

_____

_____

_____

_____

Practice reading the passage and record yourself again. Then complete the evaluation below.

My reading was:	very smooth	somewhat smooth	choppy
My reading rate was:	too fast	too slow	just right

I made mistakes reading these words:

_____

_____

Did I use expression?   Yes   No

Here is how my reading fluency changed:

_____

_____

_____

_____

_____

Partner Reading Activities

Reading in Pairs

Standards: 5.1, 5.9, and 5.10

Paired student reading is another way that students can practice fluency.

Materials

- copy of the partner reading chart below
- two-pocket folder
- reading passage
- pencils
- copies of page 89

1. Think about combinations of students who you think will work well together. You may choose a mixed ability group so a struggling reader can hear a fluent reader. You might also pair students with equal abilities.
2. Instruct students to set common goals and work together to read with fluency.
3. Provide students with copies of the form below.
4. Have each student place the form in a reading folder.
5. After each partner reading, each student should complete the form.
6. As an additional activity, have students complete the activity on page 89.

Partner Reading Chart

Date: _____

My partner was _____

The book we read was _____

We did a great job on _____

_____

We need to improve on _____

Date: _____

My partner was _____

The book we read was _____

We did a great job on _____

_____

We need to improve on _____

Date: _____

My partner was _____

The book we read was _____

We did a great job on _____

_____

We need to improve on _____

Pair Reading Chart

1. Select a partner.
2. Choose a passage to read aloud to your partner.
3. Read the passage aloud three times.
4. Have your partner complete the form below after your second and third readings.

	Second Reading	Third Reading
Improved Accuracy		
Read Faster		
Read Smoother		
Read with Better Expression		

Write two compliments about your partner's reading fluency.

_____

_____

Write one suggestion for your partner to practice.

_____

_____

Partner Reading Activities *(cont.)*

Reading Rate

Standard: 5.10

This activity will help your students understand what is meant by a "comfortable reading rate."

Materials

- tape recorder with microphone and headphones
- cassette tape

1. When telling students to read at a comfortable reading rate, it might be difficult for them to understand what this means.
2. Explain that when people speak in regular conversation, they speak between 130 and 160 words per minute.
3. Have them test this by working in pairs to record themselves telling a story about a recent event. The student should speak for exactly one minute.
4. At the end of the minute, the students work together to count the number of words the student said in one minute.
5. Once it is determined that the conversational rate was between 130 and 160 words per minute, have the students replay the recording, paying attention to the rate of speech.
6. Draw attention to the fact that the rate is neither too fast nor too slow, but that we usually read a bit slower than we speak. This should serve as a guide for a comfortable reading rate.

Goal Setting

Standard: 5.10

Have your students work to set and attain goals for their reading rate. You can teach your students to work together to assist one another with reading fluency.

Materials

- stop watch
- markers or colored pencils
- copy of Peer Tutoring Instructions (page 92)

1. Explain to the students that they will take on either the role of the tutor or the reader.
2. When the students read together, they will find a place to sit that is away from other student pairs.
3. The reader reads aloud for five minutes and tries to read at a comfortable rate, with expression, and without making mistakes.
4. The tutor is instructed to be a good listener and pay attention to the student's reading rate, accuracy, and expression.
5. If a mistake is made by the reader, the tutor draws attention to the word, reads it aloud, and asks the reader to repeat it.
6. When the reader completes reading for five minutes, the two exchange roles and repeat the process.
7. On page 92, you will find an instruction sheet that can be posted to assist tutors and readers as they work together.

Goal Setting—Words Per Minute

Use this page to track your progress with improving your reading rate.

1. Begin by finding a baseline reading rate. Do this by having a classmate time your reading for one minute.
2. Have your partner time your reading two more times. Each time, count the number of words you were able to read in one minute.
3. Record your progress on the graph by coloring on the corresponding block.
4. Set a goal for improving your reading rate. For example, if your timed readings were 60, 62, and 65 words per minute, you might want to set a goal of increasing your reading rate to 70 words per minute.

Name:	Date:		
	First Reading	**Second Reading**	**Third Reading**
150			
140			
130			
120			
110			
100			
90			
80			
70			
60			
50			
40			
30			

Peer Tutoring Instructions

Find a place to sit where you will not be distracted.

Reader

✧ Read aloud for five minutes.

✧ Try to read at a comfortable reading rate.

✧ Try to read with expression.

✧ Try to read without making mistakes.

Tutor

✧ Be a good listener.

✧ Pay attention to the reader's reading rate, accuracy, and expression.

✧ If the reader makes a mistake, point to the word and read it aloud.

✧ Ask the reader to repeat the word and continue.

Readers Theater

Readers Theater

Standards: 5.9, 5.10

What Is Readers Theater?

Readers Theater is a fun way for children to practice oral reading with fluency. There are many ways it can be implemented in the classroom.

✧ **Teacher/Group Reading**—for this kind of Readers Theater, the teacher has the primary reading role. The script contains repetitive parts that the children join in on.

✧ **Quick Scripts**—with quick scripts, the children practice short readings on different occasions. The scripts are reintroduced, periodically, for fluency practice.

✧ **Rehearsed Reading for Performance**—these can involve short or long scripts that the children practice for the purpose of performing for the class.

How to Begin

Children need to understand the purpose of Readers Theater. Gather them together in a group and read a short passage from a familiar story such as *The Three Little Pigs*. Discuss the events of the story. Ask them how the pigs might have felt.

- How would the pigs speak to the wolf?
- Were they frightened?
- Were they angry?
- How would their voices sound when they spoke?
- How would the wolf's voice sound when he spoke to the pigs?

Invite students to recite dialog from *The Three Little Pigs* using appropriate expression. Explain that when performing Readers Theater, it is important to assume the role of the character and speak in the same way that the character would speak.

Important Tips

- Always allow children to review and practice scripts before reading aloud.
- Encourage the children to use expression when they read.
- Encourage the children to read as smoothly as possible.
- Allow time for the children to rehearse their lines before a performance.

Readers Theater Activities

Be a Script Writer

Standard: 5.9

This activity allows your students to create their own Readers Theater scripts to assist with reading fluency.

Materials

- reading passage (with dialog)
- chart paper
- marker
- copies of Planning Sheet (page 95)
- copies of Script Writing Sheet (page 96)

1. Draw students' attention to the characters included in the dialog, and have them determine whether or not the passage would require a narrator.

2. Write the script on chart paper, writing a character's name and the dialog he or she says.

3. Explain that for a Readers Theater performance, a person has to be selected for each character and the narrator.

4. Duplicate pages 95–96 and have students use the Planning Sheet (page 95) as a guide. Then have them use the Script Writing Sheet (page 96) to record the script for the Readers Theater performance.

Story Summaries

Standard: 5.9

Another way to have students create their own Readers Theater scripts is to have them summarize stories and create their own dialog.

Materials

- copies of Planning Sheet (page 95)
- copies of Script Writing Sheet (page 96)

1. Rather than taking dialog straight from the story, students recall the most important events and dialog exchanges and then write a script that summarizes the story.

2. Have the students write the script in the same manner described above with each character's name and dialog beside it.

3. The students can use the Planning Sheet and Script Writing Sheet (pages 95–96) to guide them through the process.

Planning Sheet

Name of Book: _____

Roles

Character   **Student Actor**

_____   _____

_____   _____

_____   _____

_____   _____

_____   _____

Narrator:

_____

Script Writers:

_____

_____

_____

Describe your strategy for rehearsal.

_____

_____

_____

_____

_____

Script Writing Sheet

Name of Book: _____

Story Setting: _____

Beginning of the Story

Character   Line

_____ : _____

_____ : _____

_____ : _____

_____ : _____

_____ : _____

Middle of the Story

Character   Line

_____ : _____

_____ : _____

_____ : _____

_____ : _____

_____ : _____

End of the Story

Character   Line

_____ : _____

_____ : _____

_____ : _____

_____ : _____

Assessment

Reading Level Calculation

According to *Put Reading First* (2001, p. 29), you can calculate correct words per minute with the formula explained below.

Materials

- two reading passages at the third grade level
- copy of Fluency Graph (page 99)
- stop watch or clock with second hand

1. Select two passages of text at the third grade level (not reading level).
2. Have a student read a passage for one minute.
3. Count the number of words the child read in one minute.
4. Determine the number of words read incorrectly.
5. Repeat the steps above with the second passage.
6. Determine the average number of words read incorrectly per minute.
7. Subtract the number of errors from the total number of words read to determine the words correct per minute (WCPM).
8. Repeat this process a few times during the school year to assess each student's progress. The chart below can be used as a guideline for average fluency goals.
9. Use the graph on page 99 to record student progress.

Average Fluency Goals

- 60 WCPM = end of first grade
- 114 WCPM = end of third grade

Word-Processing Reading Level Tool

Some word-processing programs have reading level tools that you can use to determine the level of a passage.

Materials

- word-processing program with a reading level tool
- reading passage

1. To use this tool in Microsoft Word, you will need to turn it on.
2. Click on the Tools menu at the top of the screen and select Preferences (or Options).
3. Click on the Spelling & Grammar tab from the resulting window.
4. Then click to make a check mark beside Show Readability Statistics and click OK.
5. Highlight a passage of text and then click on the Tools Menu.
6. Select Spelling & Grammar.
7. After the program runs a spell check, click on okay and a window will appear.
8. At the bottom of this window, you will see the Flesch-Kincaid Grade Level. The grade level of the passage will be listed beside it. (If you have a word-processing program other than Microsoft Word, search the Help tool of your program for a readability tool. Follow the instructions for your word-processing program.)

Fluency Four-Point Rubric

Use this rubric to assist with assessing your student's fluency progress.

4	The student reads with appropriate phrasing. Very few mistakes are made and do not take away from the meaning of the passage. The student reads expressively throughout all or most of the passage.
3	The student generally reads with appropriate phrasing. Some mistakes are made with word pronunciation. The student attempts to read with expression.
2	The student reads in two- to four-word phrases. Some word pronunciation mistakes are made. The student does not read with expression.
1	The student reads word-by-word, makes frequent mistakes in pronunciation, and does not use expression.

Fluency Graph

Use the graph below to track a student's fluency progress. Calculate words correct per minute (see page 97) and record fluency readings throughout the year. This will provide a visual record of progress to show to parents. For each assessment, first plot the words read per minute (Words); then plot the words correct per minute (WCPM).

	Words	WCPM	Words	WCPM	Words	WCPM	Words	WCPM
150								
140								
130								
120								
110								
100								
90								
80								
70								
60								
50								
40								
30								
20								
	Date:		Date:		Date:		Date:	

Vocabulary

In order to communicate effectively, we need to have an adequate vocabulary. This is typically thought of as oral vocabulary and reading vocabulary, but also includes listening and writing vocabulary. *Reading vocabulary* is the words we recognize when we read. *Oral vocabulary* is the words we use and understand when speaking. *Listening vocabulary* is the words we understand when listening to others speak. *Writing vocabulary* is the words we use in our own writing.

Why Is Vocabulary Important?

Instruction in this area is important because vocabulary helps children make sense of print, increases their comprehension, and enables them to understand more difficult texts.

Indirect Vocabulary Learning

Vocabulary can be taught directly or indirectly. However, most vocabulary is learned indirectly. It happens as we communicate through speaking and writing in everyday life. When we hear or see words used in different concepts, it helps us to expand our knowledge of word meanings. This book provides indirect vocabulary activities for daily oral language, adult read aloud, and independent reading.

Direct Vocabulary Learning

Some vocabulary is learned directly. This involves explicit instruction of individual words. While most vocabulary is learned indirectly, direct vocabulary instruction can improve children's reading comprehension. Direct vocabulary learning involves specific-word instruction and word-learning strategies.

Specific-Word Instruction

With specific-word instruction, students are taught individual words and their meanings. This is typically done to prepare students for text they will be reading. Specific-word instruction increases students' reading comprehension. It is particularly effective when children are actively involved, and helps children remember word meanings when they are used in different contexts.

Word-Learning Strategies

Because it isn't possible to teach children the meanings and pronunciations of all words they will encounter, it is important to teach children strategies to use when they encounter new words. This book provides word-learning strategies in the following areas: dictionary skills, knowledge of word parts, and using context clues.

Cautions about Vocabulary Instruction

❖ Children can be overwhelmed by vocabulary if too many words are introduced at one time. Focus only on a few words at a time.

❖ Don't spend too much time on meanings of words in isolation. This could interfere with comprehension of words in context.

❖ Don't spend too much time directly teaching vocabulary that can easily be understood in context.

❖ Remember that students need to learn what to do when they encounter new words. Be sure to spend more time teaching strategies rather than individual words.

❖ Remember that children internalize the meanings of words when they have many opportunities to encounter the words (especially in different contexts).

Synonyms and Antonyms Activities

Synonyms

Standard: 5.8

This game helps your students practice identifying synonyms.

Materials

- chalkboard and chalk
- Synonym Cards (pages 102–103)
- scissors
- resealable plastic bag

1. Write the words *keep*, *save*, and *give* on the chalkboard.
2. Ask the students to identify the two words that have similar meanings (*keep* and *save*). Explain that these two words are synonyms (they mean the same or almost the same).
3. Ask students to think of other words that are synonyms. Write these words on the chalkboard.
4. Have students practice matching synonyms by making a concentration learning center game.
5. Duplicate and cut apart the word cards on pages 102–103; store them in a plastic bag.
6. To play, a student places the cards facedown on a flat surface. The student turns over two cards at a time. If the words are synonyms, they are set to the side. If they are not synonyms, they are turned facedown again.
7. Play continues until all synonyms have been matched.

Antonyms

Standard: 5.8

Your children will have fun playing an antonym game.

Materials

- chalkboard and chalk
- paper
- pencils
- Antonym Cards (pages 104–105)
- scissors

1. Write the words *wet* and *dry* on the chalkboard. Draw attention to the fact that these words are *antonyms* (they have opposite meanings).
2. Ask the students to think of as many antonyms as possible and then write them on paper. Allow the students to share their words.
3. Duplicate and cut apart the antonym cards (pages 104–105).
4. To play, each of two players receives four cards. If a student has any words that are antonyms of each other, they make a match and set those aside.
5. In turn, each student asks for a card. For example, "Do you have a word that is the antonym of *cold*?"
6. If the student has the card, he or she hands over the card. If the student does not have it, he or she says, "Go fish."

Synonym Cards

laugh	giggle
enormous	huge
run	jog
job	career
vehicle	automobile
sick	ill

Synonym Cards *(cont.)*

carpet	**rug**
song	**tune**
cut	**slice**
animal	**creature**
healthy	**well**
obnoxious	**annoying**

Antonym Cards

win	lose
succeed	fail
tasty	bland
whisper	yell
truth	lie
smooth	bumpy

Antonym Cards *(cont.)*

slowly	**quickly**
arrive	**depart**
mend	**break**
cooked	**raw**
heavy	**light**
difficult	**easy**

General Activities

Collecting Words

Standards: 5.6, 5.8

Encourage your students to locate and define new words.

Materials
- copies of page 107
- pencils

1. Ask your students to become new word collectors. To do this, they will pay attention to unfamiliar words as they read on their own.

2. Provide each student with the word collection sheet on page 107.

3. When a student finds a new word, he or she records it on the sheet and then writes how the word is used. The student also attempts to define the word and uses it in a different sentence.

4. Periodically allow students to share the words they have found.

Words in Conversation

Standards: 5.6, 5.8

Help your students add new words to their conversational vocabulary.

Materials
- index cards
- pencils
- hole puncher
- metal rings

1. As your students find and define new words, encourage them to use these words in their spoken language.

2. Periodically have students review their word collections (see activity above).

3. Instruct each student to select two or three words. The student reviews each word's meaning and then tries to use each one in a sentence.

4. Have the student write each word on a different index card.

5. Then have the student use a hole puncher to punch a hole in the top right corner of each card.

6. The student then places the cards on a metal ring.

7. Tell the students to try to use their new words a few times in the coming week.

8. Have them continue to add words each week to the metal ring and praise the students when they are able to use their selected words in conversation.

Word Collection

Name: _____

The word I found: _____

The sentence using the word: _____

Definition: _____

A new sentence using the word: _____

The word I found: _____

The sentence using the word: _____

Definition: _____

A new sentence using the word: _____

The word I found: _____

The sentence using the word: _____

Definition: _____

A new sentence using the word: _____

The word I found: _____

The sentence using the word: _____

Definition: _____

A new sentence using the word: _____

The word I found: _____

The sentence using the word: _____

Definition: _____

A new sentence using the word: _____

The word I found: _____

The sentence using the word: _____

Definition: _____

A new sentence using the word: _____

General Activitiess *(cont.)*

Finding Nouns and Adjectives

Standard: 5.8

Use this activity to help your students identify new nouns and adjectives.

Materials

- chalkboard and chalk
- reading passage with some unfamiliar words
- paper
- pencils

1. Review nouns and adjectives with your students. Explain that a *noun* is a word that represents a person, place, or thing. Explain that an *adjective* is a word that describes a person, place, or thing.
2. Write the following sentence on the chalkboard:

    The small jacaranda found a tasty treat to have for breakfast.
3. Ask the students to find the people, places, or things in the sentence *(jacaranda, treat, breakfast)*.
4. Then ask the students to find the words that describe these nouns *(small, tasty)*.
5. Distribute a reading passage for students to read.
6. As the students read, have them search for words that are nouns or adjectives.
7. Have them list these words on paper.
8. Allow the students to share the words they found and discuss their meanings.

Word Wall Game

Standards: 5.6, 5.8

Here's a fun game to play while creating a word wall in your classroom.

Materials

- construction-paper squares or index cards   • marker   • stapler

1. As your students identify new vocabulary words, use a marker to write them on construction-paper squares or index cards.
2. Staple the word cards to the wall and review the pronunciations and meanings frequently.
3. Periodically play a word wall game to make word learning fun.
4. Secretly select a word from the wall (for example, *elevate*) and tell the students a riddle about it, such as:

> This word means to raise up.   This word rhymes with renovate.

5. Continue in this manner with other words on the word wall.

General Activities *(cont.)*

Word Introduction

Standards: 5.6, 5.8

When introducing new stories to your students, it is important to help students understand words that are unfamiliar.

Materials

- children's literature book
- marker
- sentence strips

1. Before introducing a new book to your students, read through it to identify words that might be difficult for your students to pronounce or understand.
2. Write each word on a different piece of sentence strip. (Choose no more than eight words.)
3. Then write the definition of each word on a separate piece of sentence strip.
4. Finally, write a sentence using each word on separate sentence strips.
5. Gather students in a small group and introduce them to the vocabulary words.
6. Ask the students if they know any of the words.
7. Then display each strip with a sentence on it. Read the sentences aloud and ask the students if they are able to define the vocabulary words based on how they are used in sentences.
8. Finally, show the students the definition strips and ask the students to match the definitions to the words they attempted to define.

Vocabulary Presentations

Standards: 5.6, 5.7, and 5.8

This activity involves students in defining new words.

Materials

- children's literature book
- pencils
- paper
- dictionary (optional)

1. In a small group, have students work together to help one another learn new words.
2. Provide students with children's literature.
3. Ask each student to skim through the book to locate two or three words that might be unfamiliar to their group members.
4. When each child has identified two or three words, have him or her try to determine each word's meaning using context, a dictionary, or adult assistance.
5. Then the child writes a new sentence using the word correctly.
6. Finally, have each child present his or her words, definitions, and sentences to the other children in the group.

General Activities *(cont.)*

Word Substitutions

Standards: 5.6, 5.8

This activity will help your students relate new vocabulary words to words they already know.

Materials

- index cards
- marker

1. When students are introduced to new words, it is often helpful to relate new words to words they already know.
2. Select the new words students will encounter in text and then think of common words that are synonyms to these.
3. Write a new word on one side of an index card and a common synonym on the other side of the card.
4. Introduce the students to each new word and ask them if they know the word's meaning.
5. Then show them the synonym to the word.
6. Provide students with examples of the words used in sentences and show them how to interchange the words with their synonyms to gain greater understanding of the new vocabulary.
7. Place the word cards in a learning center and encourage the students to review them periodically.

Definition Collages

Standard: 5.8

With this activity, your students create visual definitions of vocabulary words.

Materials

- chart paper
- marker
- magazines
- scissors
- glue
- construction paper

1. Have your students think of creative ways to define new words.
2. First, select the words to define and write them on chart paper along with their definitions.
3. Provide your students with magazines, scissors, and glue and explain to them that they will try to find magazine illustrations that represent the meaning of the word. For example, explain that if one of the words was *transparent*, the students might find magazine pictures of windows, clear dishes, clear plastic wrap, etc.
4. Provide each student in the group with a sheet of construction paper and designate two words for him or her to define using pictures.
5. The student writes each word on one side of the construction paper and then creates a collage of pictures that define the word on the other side.
6. When students are finished with their collages, instruct them to take turns sharing them and explain why they chose the pictures they did.

Daily Oral Language Activities

Idioms

Standard: 5.8

Materials

- idiom cards (pages 112–115)
- wipe-off marker
- scissors

1. Explain that an *idiom* is a phrase that has one meaning when it is typically used in our language, but it can have a funny meaning. For example: *It's raining cats and dogs.* In our language this means that figuratively it's raining really hard, but literally it would mean that cats and dogs are falling from the sky.

2. Duplicate, cut apart, and laminate the idiom cards (pages 112–115).

3. Have students look at the picture and idiom on one of the cards and then write two sentences on the lines using a wipe-off marker. The first sentence should explain the figurative meaning of the idiom and the second sentence should explain the literal meaning.

> **Example:** Turn right at the fork in the road.
>
> **Sentence 1:** When the road splits into two, take the road on the right.
>
> **Sentence 2:** When you see a fork lying in the road, turn right.

Nonsense Words

Standard: 5.8

Materials

- chalkboard and chalk

Write the sentence below on the chalkboard and ask the students to read it silently.

The red cxoijg drove down the road slowly.

Draw attention to the nonsense word. Tell the students that this is not a real word, but the way it is used in the sentence might give us a clue as to what the word should be. Ask the following questions:

> Where is the *cxoijg?*   What is it doing?
>
> Do you think it is a living thing?   What verb gives a clue about what it is?

Lead the students to understand that the nonsense word is probably some kind of vehicle. The word drove and the fact that it is in the street are clues that indicate this. Continue to practice with defining nonsense words using the sentences below.

The hwoei sang sweetly from the treetop.

I'm hungry for sldiu with chocolate syrup.

The woeih blew out the candle.

The sky was woeireg. There wasn't a cloud to be seen.

Idiom Cards

Cut it out!

It's time to hit the hay.

Idiom Cards *(cont.)*11

I've got my eye on you.

I'm feeling under the weather.

Idiom Cards *(cont.)*

Don't blow your top.

Zip your lip!

Idiom Cards *(cont.)*

It cost an arm and a leg.

I'm so hungry I could eat a horse.

Adult Read-Aloud Activities

Slang

Standard: 5.8

Understanding the use of slang is important for a few reasons. First, children need to recognize slang spellings versus the proper spellings of words. Second, children need to understand when slang is and is not appropriate.

Materials

- copies of page 117
- pencils

1. Discuss slang words, such as *gotcha, lemme,* and *ain't*. Explain that when writing formally, slang is inappropriate.
2. Continue practice by having each child complete page 117.

Story Time Vocabulary

Standard: 5.6

Story time is the perfect time to address new words encountered in children's literature.

Materials

- chapter book
- word list

1. Explain to the children that it is common to encounter new words when listening to the teacher read during story time.
2. Instruct the students to raise their hands when they hear unfamiliar words.
3. Then take a minute to discuss the word's meaning, trying to determine the definition based on how it is used in the sentence.
4. You might also wish to point out particular words to students. Just be sure not to focus too much time on vocabulary discussion, as the enjoyment of the story could be lost.
5. See the list below for two popular chapter books and vocabulary words that could be used for discussion.

Chapter Books and Vocabulary

The books below are great read-alouds for third grade. Below each title is a list of vocabulary words featured in the story that can be used for discussion.

Stone Fox by John Reynolds Gardiner

Chapter 1	Chapter 4
examination	derringer
Chapter 2	Chapter 6
irrigation	cunning
bushel	reservation
acre	

Maniac Magee by Jerry Spinelli

Chapter 3	Chapter 15
suspicious	vacant
Chapter 5	Chapter 22
misfortune	scrawny
Chapter 7	
beeline	

Find the Slang

Read each sentence below and determine whether or not slang is used. Write **Slang** if the sentence uses a slang word. Write **No Slang** if the sentence uses proper English. On the line below each sentence that uses slang, rewrite the sentence using proper English.

1. Lemme see what's happening!_____

_____

2. Hey, Tim, wassup? _____

_____

3. You're such a nice person. _____

_____

4. You gotta help me with my homework._____

_____

5. Have you seen the movie yet? _____

_____

6. I'm gonna go on a trip next week. _____

_____

7. Gimme the toy, please._____

_____

8. That was, like, so fun!_____

_____

9. Thanks for the gift. _____

_____

10. Don't get upset. Just chill out! _____

_____

Specific-Word Instruction Activities

Independent Reading

Standard: 5.7

Assist your students in determining the meanings of new words as they read silently.

Materials

- copies of the independent reading form below
- pencils
- reading passages
- dictionaries

1. Provide each child with a copy of the form below.

2. In the first column, the child writes a new word found in the text.

3. Next, the student writes the sentence that included the word.

4. Finally, the student looks up the word in the dictionary and writes the definition. Be sure the student writes the definition of the word as it is used in the sentence.

Independent Reading Form		
Word	**Sentence**	**Definition**

Specific-Word Instruction Activities *(cont.)*

Word Detectives

Standard: 5.8

Use this activity to introduce new vocabulary words from a selected book.

Materials

- children's literature book
- paper
- pencils

1. Provide a copy of a selected children's book for each student.
2. Ask students to look through the book in search of unfamiliar words.
3. Ask them to make a list of the words as they find them.
4. Have them share the list with the class. Help students defiine the words.

Using Context to Define Words

Standard: 5.6

This activity teaches students how to use context to determine a word's meaning.

Material

- children's literature book

1. Provide a copy of a selected children's book for each student and ask them to search for unfamiliar words.
2. Have the students read the word in the sentence.
3. Ask them if the sentence provides any clues as to the word's meaning.
4. Direct the students to read surrounding sentences to determine the meaning of the word.

Play Cards

Standard: 5.8

Here's another way to introduce story words.

Materials

- children's literature book
- index cards
- marker

1. Before having your students read the book, review some of the difficult words they will encounter.
2. Write each word on an index card.
3. Review the words one by one, asking the children to pronounce each one and try to use it in a sentence.

Specific-Word Instruction *(cont.)*

Which Word?

Standard: 5.6

This is a fun game for identifying the meanings of words.

Material

- short children's literature book

1. Instruct the students to read the book at least one time.
2. Tell the students that you will give clues about a word in the book, and that they need to find the word you are describing.
3. Give a clue such as, "The word I'm thinking of is a synonym for *gigantic*."
4. The students look through the book to try to locate the word being described.

What Does It Mean?

Standard: 5.8

Reinforce newly encountered words from a children's literature book with this activity.

Materials

- pencils and papers
- copies of teacher prepared worksheet

1. Create a worksheet that provides practice of new vocabulary words.
2. To prepare the worksheet, write a paragraph using the new vocabulary words.
3. Be sure to underline each featured word.
4. The student determines each word's meaning and writes a definition of it.

A Different Way

Standard: 5.6

Understanding new words can be easier when they are used in different sentences.

Materials

- children's literature book
- marker
- chart paper

1. Tell the students that words can be used in different contexts.
2. After reading a book, draw attention to the new vocabulary words they learned.
3. Write these words on chart paper and ask the students to think of sentences using the words. Write these sentences on chart paper as well. Ask the students for two or three sentences for each word.

Specific-Word Instruction *(cont.)*

Freeze!

Standards: 5.2, 5.8

Here's a lively game to help your students learn new vocabulary words.

Materials

- copy of page 122
- scissors
- index cards
- glue

1. Duplicate and cut apart the cards on page 122.
2. Glue each word card onto an index card for durability.
3. Choose five students to select one word card each.
4. Each student thinks of a way to represent the word in a pose. For example, with the word *skyscraper*, the student might stand tall with his or her arms overhead.
5. To play the game, have the other classmates sit in a circle.
6. The five selected students walk around inside the circle.
7. Say the word, *"Freeze!"*
8. The students in the circle freeze in the pose that represents the word.
9. Ask the classmates to guess each student's word before the actor shows them the word card.
10. If the students have difficulty guessing the word, they can say, *"Unfreeze."*
11. At this point, the student begins to move to act out the word.
12. Continue in this manner, selecting five new students.

Guess My Word

Standard: 5.8

This guessing game helps children practice their word knowledge.

Materials

- list of recently introduced vocabulary words
- marker
- chart paper

1. Write the selected vocabulary words on chart paper.
2. Select a student to begin the game.
3. The student chooses a word from the list and then creates a clue. The clue should include an antonym, synonym, or definition of the word.

> Example for the word *beautiful:*
> I'm thinking of a word that is a synonym for *pretty.*
> I'm thinking of a word that is an antonym for *ugly.*

4. Allow students to guess the word.
5. The student who guesses the word correctly gets to give the next clue.

Word Cards

mountain	skyscraper
automobile	suitcase
tornado	bouquet
curtains	excited
frighten	whistle

Word-Learning Strategies Activities

Independent Reading Guide

Standard: 5.1, 5.6, 5.7

This activity allows students to skim text before reading to identify new words.

Materials

- reading material
- pencils
- copies of independent reading guide (page 124)

1. Explain to students that sometimes when reading, we encounter new words. Further explain that good readers use strategies to determine the meanings of these words. Readers often use the following strategies to determine word meaning:

> - pictures in a story
> - how the word is used in a story (context)
> - dictionary

2. Have each student select a book to read.
3. Provide each student with a copy of page 124.
4. Before reading the book, instruct each student to skim the text to look for unfamiliar words. The student records each new word on the reading guide.
5. Then instruct the student to read the story. As each new word is encountered while reading, the child selects a method of determining its meaning.
6. The student places an X in the box that indicates the selected strategy, and then writes a definition of the word.

Personal Dictionary

Standard: 5.7

Learning to use the dictionary is a difficult, but necessary, skill for third graders. Help the students understand the need for dictionaries by providing them with their own mini-dictionaries to add new words.

Materials

- copies of Personal Dictionary (pages 125–130)
- stapler
- scissors
- pencils

1. Duplicate pages 125–130 for each student.
2. Instruct the students to cut apart the pages and assemble them into mini-dictionaries.
3. Draw students' attention to the blanks on each page and explain that these lines are provided for them to add new words and their meanings.
4. Explain that as they encounter new words they should select a method of determining the words' meanings. The students record the words and their definitions in the dictionaries.
5. Encourage the students to refer to their personal dictionaries as they encounter these new words again and to add new words often.

Independent Reading Guide

Book Title: _____	Pictures	Context	Dictionary	Other
Word: Definition:				
Word: Definition:				
Word: Definition:				
Word: Definition:				
Word: Definition:				
Word: Definition:				
Word: Definition:				
Word: Definition:				
Word: Definition:				

Personal Dictionary

A	
Words	Definitions
————	————————
————	————————
————	————————
————	————————
————	————————
————	————————

B	
Words	Definitions
————	————————
————	————————
————	————————
————	————————
————	————————
————	————————

C	
Words	Definitions
————	————————
————	————————
————	————————
————	————————
————	————————

D	
Words	Definitions
————	————————
————	————————
————	————————
————	————————
————	————————

Personal Dictionary *(cont.)*

E

Words	Definitions
_____	_____
_____	_____
_____	_____
_____	_____
_____	_____
_____	_____

F

Words	Definitions
_____	_____
_____	_____
_____	_____
_____	_____
_____	_____
_____	_____

G

Words	Definitions
_____	_____
_____	_____
_____	_____
_____	_____
_____	_____
_____	_____

H

Words	Definitions
_____	_____
_____	_____
_____	_____
_____	_____
_____	_____
_____	_____

Personal Dictionary *(cont.)*

I

Words	Definitions
_____	_____
_____	_____
_____	_____
_____	_____
_____	_____
_____	_____

J

Words	Definitions
_____	_____
_____	_____
_____	_____
_____	_____
_____	_____
_____	_____

K

Words	Definitions
_____	_____
_____	_____
_____	_____
_____	_____
_____	_____

L

Words	Definitions
_____	_____
_____	_____
_____	_____
_____	_____
_____	_____

Personal Dictionary *(cont.)*

M	
Words	Definitions
_____	_____
_____	_____
_____	_____
_____	_____
_____	_____
_____	_____

N	
Words	Definitions
Words	Definitions
_____	_____
_____	_____
_____	_____
_____	_____
_____	_____

O	
Words	Definitions
_____	_____
_____	_____
_____	_____
_____	_____
_____	_____

P	
Words	Definitions
_____	_____
_____	_____
_____	_____
_____	_____
_____	_____

Personal Dictionary *(cont.)*

Q

Words	Definitions
_____	_____
_____	_____
_____	_____
_____	_____
_____	_____
_____	_____

R

Words	Definitions
_____	_____
_____	_____
_____	_____
_____	_____
_____	_____
_____	_____

S

Words	Definitions
_____	_____
_____	_____
_____	_____
_____	_____
_____	_____

T

Words	Definitions
_____	_____
_____	_____
_____	_____
_____	_____
_____	_____

Personal Dictionary *(cont.)*

U

Words   Definitions

_____   _____

_____   _____

V

Words   Definitions

_____   _____

_____   _____

X

Words   Definitions

_____   _____

_____   _____

Y

Words   Definitions

_____   _____

_____   _____

W

Words   Definitions

_____   _____

_____   _____

_____   _____

_____   _____

_____   _____

Z

Words   Definitions

_____   _____

_____   _____

_____   _____

_____   _____

_____   _____

Word-Learning Strategies Activities *(cont.)*

Dictionary Skills

Standard: 5.7

Using a dictionary is an important skill for third graders, but it can be difficult without practice.

Materials

- dictionaries
- copies of page 132
- pencils

1. Provide students with dictionaries to look through.
2. Ask them to identify the uses of a dictionary, such as spelling words correctly, defining words, determining parts of speech, locating synonyms for words, etc.
3. Draw students' attention to the guide words at the top of the pages. Explain that these words indicate the first and last words found on the page of a dictionary. All the other words on the page are sequenced alphabetically between them. For example, if the guide words are *car* and *cat*, the word cart might be found on the page, but the word *cent* would not because "ce-" comes after "ca-", alphabetically.
4. Have students practice using guide words by completing page 132.

Thesaurus

Standards: 5.7, 5.8

Your students can practice using a thesaurus with these activities.

Materials

- thesauri
- copies of pages 133–134
- pencils

1. Display a thesaurus for your students and ask them if they know its purpose and how it is used.
2. Explain that a *thesaurus* is used to find synonyms and antonyms of words. For example, a thesaurus that features the word *angry* might list the following words as synonyms and antonyms:

Synonyms	Antonyms
annoyed	calm
irritated	peaceful
mad	tranquil
irate	

3. Have students practice using a thesaurus by completing pages 133–134.

Guide Words

Guide words at the top of dictionary pages will help you find words. Look at each set of guide words and circle the word that would be found on that page.

1. able　•　add

apple　　ask　　act

2. bottle　•　break

boss　　bow　　balance

3. trick　•　tumble

trust　　twist　　track

4. pie　•　plate

please　　pencil　　place

5. severe　•　shape

share　　seven　　shame

6. well　•　wise

waste　　wiggle　　wobble

7. ghost　•　glow

glad　　gone　　great

8. cry　•　custard

crust　　cloud　　cuff

Using a Thesaurus

Read each sentence below. Look up the **boldfaced** word in a thesaurus. Rewrite the sentence using a **synonym** for the boldfaced word.

1. Tracy has **blonde** hair.

2. I bought new **clothes** for school.

3. We have a big tree in front of our **house**.

4. What did you eat for **dinner**?

5. A big **storm** is coming.

6. Will your mom **prepare** breakfast for us?

7. I hate to do **chores**.

8. My cat is so **cute**.

9. Is that your **car**?

10. Tomorrow I am going on **vacation.**

Using a Computer Thesaurus

Most word-processing programs include a thesaurus that can be useful from locating synonyms and antonyms for words. Determine how to use the thesaurus with your word-processing program.

- Using Microsoft® Word X, the thesaurus is found in the Tools menu.
- Using older versions of Word, the thesaurus is found by first clicking Tools and then moving the cursor down to Language.

Use the Thesaurus tool to find synonyms and antonyms for each word below. Then write them in the correct space. (If no antonyms are listed, write **None**.)

Word	Synonyms	Antonyms
1. happy		
2. cold		
3. laugh		
4. heavy		
5. important		
6. sick		
7. cry		
8. rich		

Comprehension

What is reading without understanding? Reading is, first and foremost, a meaning-making process. Without comprehension reading is not reading.

Purpose

Reading is about purpose. Sometime we read to locate information. Other times we read for enjoyment. Good readers know that the process of reading involves purpose.

Thinking

Good readers think as they read. They concentrate on the storyline, vocabulary, and making sense of the text.

Why Is Comprehension Instruction Important?

According to the National Reading Panel's report, research suggests that instruction of comprehension strategies helps children become more purposeful, active readers. They make use of prior knowledge to connect new information with information that is already known, as well as using visual images to form mental pictures that make written material more meaningful. Effective instruction in this area involves:

- monitoring
- using graphic organizers
- answering questions
- generating questions
- recognizing story structure
- summarizing

Monitoring Comprehension

There are many ways that students can monitor their own comprehension, including:

- identifying unfamiliar words
- identifying information that is not understood
- clarifying new understanding
- reviewing information featured in text
- searching to clarify information in text

Graphic Organizers

Graphic or semantic organizers are visual representations of concepts and ideas. These can be in the form of maps, webs, clusters, charts, or graphs. Graphic organizers assist readers with:

- identifying a purpose for reading
- organizing thoughts about written information

Comprehension *(cont.)*

Answering Questions

Questioning strategies are helpful in the development of comprehension. By using questioning strategies, teachers can effectively monitor their students' comprehension. Questioning assists in the following ways:

- providing purpose for reading
- focusing students' attention on meaning
- encouraging thinking while reading
- reviewing what was read

Generating Questions

Comprehension can also be increased by teaching children to ask their own questions about text. When generating questions about text, students use metacognitive strategies that confirm the things they do and do not understand when reading.

Recognizing Story Structure

When students understand story structure, they have knowledge of how events are organized to form the plot of a story. This knowledge leads to better story recall and understanding. Story maps and other kinds of graphic organizers can be used with instruction of story structure to clarify story content. Instruction in this area involves:

- setting
- events
- characters
- plot

Summarizing

When students summarize stories, they must have enough understanding about a piece of text to condense the main ideas into just a few sentences. Summarizing involves the use of the following skills:

- identifying main ideas
- connecting ideas
- removing insignificant details
- story recall

This section of the book provides activities that focus on monitoring, using graphic organizers, answering questions, generating questions, understanding story structure, and summarizing. In addition to these, you will find tools for comprehension assessment.

Monitoring Comprehension Activities

Metacognition

Standard: 5.9

Metacognition involves a person's ability to think about his or her own thinking. For example, if a person thinks about a particular topic, he or she would use metacognitive strategies to identify the things he or she does and does not know about it.

Materials

- reference materials
- copies of page 138
- pencils

1. Explain to the students that when learning about a topic, it is important to identify what you know and what you do not know. The things we don't know, but would like to learn, often guide our research.
2. Distribute copies of page 138 and have each student write a topic of interest in the designated area on the chart.
3. Have the student complete the chart by listing the things he or she does know and the things he or she does not know.
4. Allow each student to use reference materials to locate new information about the topic. Have the student write this new information on the chart.

Cause and Effect

Standard: 7.8

This activity encourages practice with identifying causes and effects in stories.

Materials

- chart paper
- marker
- children's book
- copies of page 139
- red and blue crayons or colored pencils

1. Begin the lesson by reviewing the meaning of cause and effect.
2. Provide an example such as, "My dad's car was filthy, but then he washed it and it was shiny and clean." Explain that washing the car was the cause that led to the effect of the car being shiny and clean.
3. Allow students to share other cause-and-effect relationships.
4. With each statement a student offers, have the students identify the cause(s) and effect(s).
5. Write these causes and effects on chart paper.
6. Read aloud a children's book and ask the students to pay attention to causes and effects.
7. As they hear causes and effects, encourage them to raise their hands and announce them to the class.
8. Continue to practice identifying causes and effects by having students complete page 139.

Metacognitive Strategy

Topic:

What I Know	What I Don't Know	What I Learned

Cause and Effect

Underline the causes in **red.** Underline the effects in **blue.**

1. I have a stomach ache because I ate too much pizza.

2. When I slipped on the ice, I bruised my hand.

3. The grass was long, so my dad mowed it.

4. Everything was white after the snowstorm.

5. My dog whined because he was hungry.

6. I forgot to water the plant, so it died.

7. When I sprinkled food into the tank, the fish came to the surface.

8. I screamed when I won the game.

9. Sally cried when she cut her finger.

10. I helped my dad clean the garage and he was happy.

Monitoring Comprehension Activities *(cont.)*

Fact or Opinion

Standard: 7.8

Materials

- chart paper and marker
- copies of pages 141–142
- pencils

1. Ask your students to think about facts about a topic, such as rainy days. List some examples on chart paper.
   - The sky is gray.
   - Many people carry umbrellas to stay dry.
   - Clouds are in the sky.
   - Usually recess is cancelled.

2. Then have the students think about their personal feelings about rainy days such as:
   - Rainy days feel cozy.
   - I love lightning and thunder.
   - Rainy days are my favorite days.
   - It is fun to watch the rain pour down from the sky.

3. Explain to the students that *facts* are true statements. Review the list in step 1 and point out that each of the sentences are true.

4. Then draw their attention to the list in step 2. Point out that these statements are not true for everyone. These are personal feelings and they are called *opinions*.

5. Have students practice identifying and creating facts and opinions by completing pages 141–142.

Facts and Opinions

Standard: 7.8

Materials

- chalkboard and chalk
- nonfiction reading material (that contains some opinions)
- paper and pencils

1. Explain to the students that when reading nonfiction we encounter many facts or things that are true. We also often encounter the author's personal feelings or opinions.

2. Write the following sentences on the chalkboard: Snow is white. Snow is cold. I love snow. Snow falls from the sky.

3. Ask the students to identify the sentences that are facts and the one sentence that represents a person's opinion.

4. Provide each student with nonfiction reading material.

5. Instruct students to read the text and list the facts and opinions on paper.

6. Have students work with partners to review their facts and opinions.

Facts and Opinions

Write two facts and two opinions for each topic below.

Facts	1. **Homework**	Opinions
	2. **Vegetables**	
	3. **Summer Vacation**	
	4. **Spiders**	
	5. **Clouds**	
	6. **The Dark**	

Fact or Opinion

Read each sentence below. Write **Fact** or **Opinion** beside each one.

A *fact* is a statement that is always true.

An *opinion* is someone's personal feeling about something.

1. Winter is a season. _____

2. Snakes are reptiles._____

3. Valentine's Day is the best day to celebrate._____

4. I love to sing. _____

5. Ice cream is cold. _____

6. Fish are better than lizards._____

7. Most plants have leaves. _____

8. Exercise is good for you. _____

9. My favorite food is lasagna._____

10. Thunderstorms are cool. _____

Monitoring Comprehension Activities *(cont.)*

Sequencing Events

Standard: 7.8

Students' abilities to sequence story events reflects their level of comprehension.

Materials

- set of written steps
- marker
- sentence strips

1. Tell your students that events in a story take place in a specific order or sequence. If these events are mixed up, the story usually doesn't make sense.
2. Write each of the events below (from *Goldilocks and the Three Bears*) on a different sentence strip.

> The bears leave their home.
> Goldilocks goes into the bears' house.
> Goldilocks tastes the porridge.
> Goldilocks tries sitting in the chairs.
> She breaks baby bear's chair.
> Goldilocks falls asleep in baby bear's bed.
> The bears come home and finds Goldilocks sleeping.

3. Mix up the sentences and display them for the students.
4. Draw students' attention to the mixed-up sequence and how this confuses the message of the story.
5. Invite the students to assist you in placing the events in the proper sequence.
6. Finally, read the sentences in the correct order.

Identifying the Main Idea

Standard: 7.5

Monitoring comprehension can be done by assessing children's abilities to identify the main idea of a story.

Materials

- children's story
- chart paper
- marker

1. Read aloud a children's story and ask the students to listen carefully.
2. Have the students name the things that happened in the story. (These do not need to be mentioned in order.)
3. Write each of these statements on chart paper.
4. When finished, review each statement and ask, "Is this what the entire story is about?"
5. Continue in this manner until the students are able to identify the one sentence that summarizes the main idea of the story.
6. Finally, write the main idea sentence and three other sentences from the list that are important for

Main Idea Activity

Finding the Main Idea

Standard: 7.5

Allow your students to continue to practice with identifying the main idea of a story.

Materials

- favorite children's books (familiar to your students)
- chart paper
- markers
- drawing paper
- crayons or markers
- copies of the Main Idea Journal (page 145)
- pencils

1. Remind the students that the *main idea* of a book is what the book is all about. For example, the main idea of the book, *A Chair for My Mother* by Vera B. Williams is that a little girl and her family save so they can buy a comfortable chair for her mother to sit in after work.

2. Explain that there are many events that happen in the story, but those are events that support the main idea.

3. Display several familiar children's books and write the title of each one on chart paper.

4. Ask the students to tell the main idea of each book using just a few sentences. Write these sentences below each title.

5. Take time to discuss the other events in each story, but point out that these are events that do not represent the main idea, but rather support the main idea.

6. Then allow the students to select familiar books from the classroom library (or books they have at home) to share with the class, identifying the main idea.

7. Distribute drawing paper and crayons or markers and have each student create an illustration that represents the main idea of the story.

8. Finally, distribute copies of page 145.

9. Explain that they will each use the reading journal to record story events and then determine the story's main idea.

10. Use the reading journal periodically to assist the students in finding the main idea.

Main Idea Journal

Book Title: _____

Important Events:

1. _____

2. _____

3. _____

4. _____

5. _____

6. _____

7. _____

8. _____

9. _____

10. _____

Write an **X** beside the two or three most important events.

Write a few sentences telling the main idea.

Main Idea:

_____

_____

_____

_____

Graphic Organizer Activities

Idea Chart

Standards: 5.2, 6.3

This graphic organizer can be used to assist children as they generate ideas about a story.

Materials

- copies of page 147
- children's story
- pencils

1. Distribute copies of page 147 to the students.
2. Explain that an idea chart is used to record events, thoughts, and questions about a story.
3. Show the students that the chart has places to write about events that happen at the beginning, middle, and end of the story. They will also write predictions, questions, and comments.
4. Instruct each student to complete the idea chart as he or she reads a new story.

Flow Chart

Standards: 5.2, 6.3

This graphic organizer can be used to assist children as they track the events of a story. A flow chart can be used to record the sequence of events in a story.

Materials

- children's stories
- copies of page 148
- pencils

1. Have each student read a short story from beginning to end.
2. Then have the student read the story again, thinking about the most important events.
3. Instruct each student to complete the Flow Chart (page 148) by sequentially listing six of the most important events in the story.

Main Idea Chart

Standards: 5.2, 7.5

This graphic organizer assists children with determining the main idea and supporting details of a story.

Materials

- children's stories
- copies of page 149
- pencils

1. After reading a children's story, have the students think about the events that took place.
2. Explain that while there are many things that happen in a story, there is usually just one main idea. The main idea is what the story is all about.
3. To complete the chart (page 149), each student thinks of several things that happen in the story.
4. Then the student determines the main idea and writes it in the designated space.
5. The student then writes the supporting details in the corresponding spaces.

Idea Chart

Book title: _____

Events at the beginning of the story:

_____

_____

What is interesting?

_____

_____

What do you think will happen next?

_____

_____

Events in the middle of the story:

_____

_____

What questions do you have?

_____

_____

Events at the end of the story:

_____

_____

Final comments about the story:

_____

_____

Flow Chart

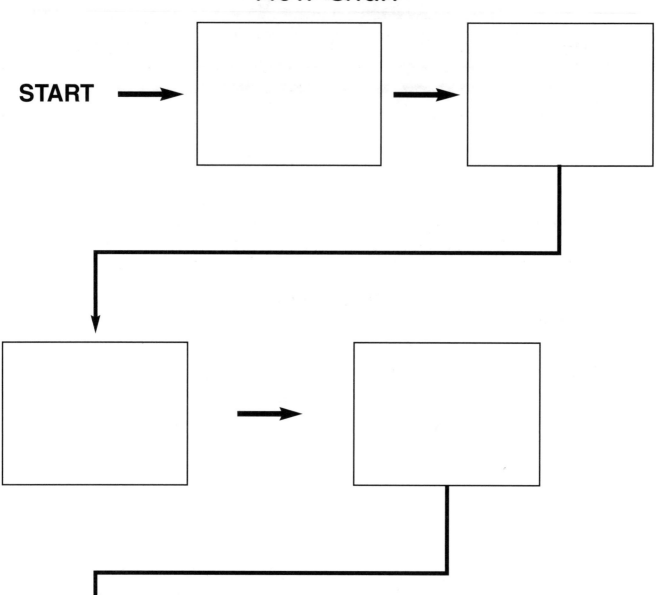

Main Idea Chart

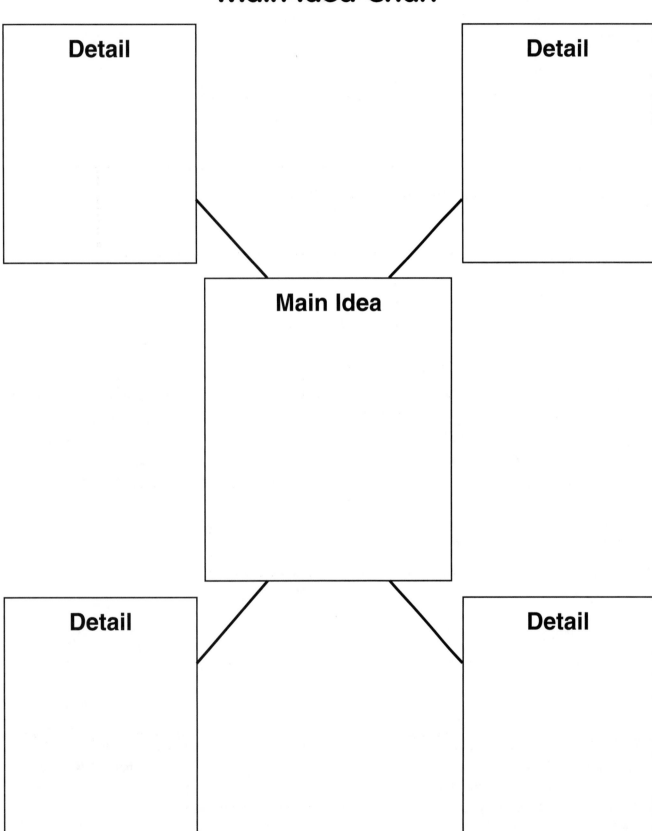

Detail

Detail

Main Idea

Detail

Detail

Graphic Organizer Activities *(cont.)*

Story Web

Standards: 5.2, 6.3

Use a story web to help students identify events in a story.

Materials

- copies of page 151
- pencils
- children's stories

1. Distribute the Story Web (page 151) and draw students' attention to the sections of the web.
2. Tell the students that they will write the title of the story in the center and important story events in the surrounding sections.
3. After completing the webs, have students discuss the events identified as most important.

Character Pyramid

Standards: 5.2, 6.5, and 6.9

This activity helps your students identify characters and their personality traits.

Materials

- copies of page 152
- pencils
- children's stories

1. Distribute the character pyramid (page 152) to the students and emphasize the different sections.
2. Explain that as they read a story, they will identify the main character and write the name of this character in the top part of the pyramid.
3. In the sections below the main character, the students write descriptions of that character.
4. In the lower portion of the pyramid, the students write the names of supporting characters and words or phrases that describe each one.
5. As an alternative use for the pyramid, students can write the characters' names and important actions or events including those characters in the story.

Story Pyramid

Standards: 5.2, 6.3, and 6.4

This activity helps your students identify specific events in a story.

Materials

- copies of page 153
- pencils
- children's stories

1. Discuss with your students different elements of a story, such as main character, setting, problem, and solution.
2. Tell the students that solving the problem in the story often involves several steps.
3. Distribute the story pyramid (page 153) to students. Identify the information that needs to be added to the pyramid, including three steps that took place in the story that led to the solution.
4. Offer guidance to the students as they complete this graphic organizer.

Story Web

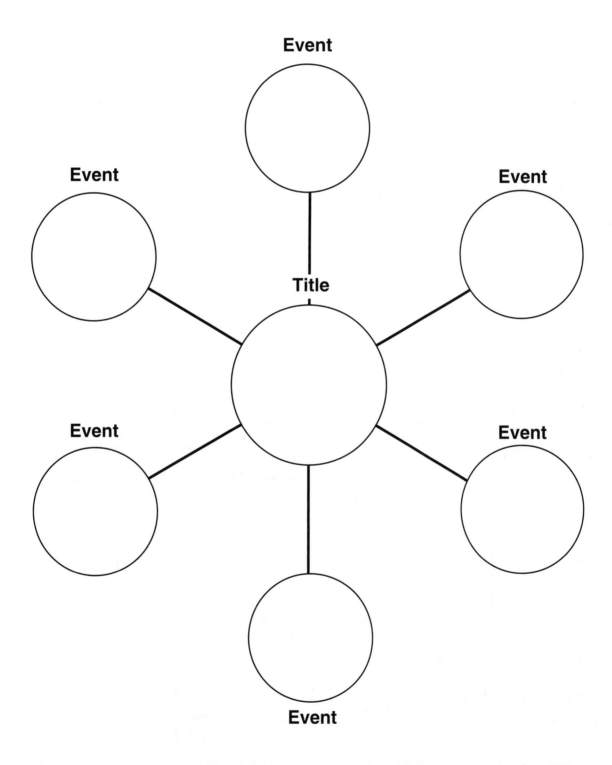

Character Pyramid

Main Character

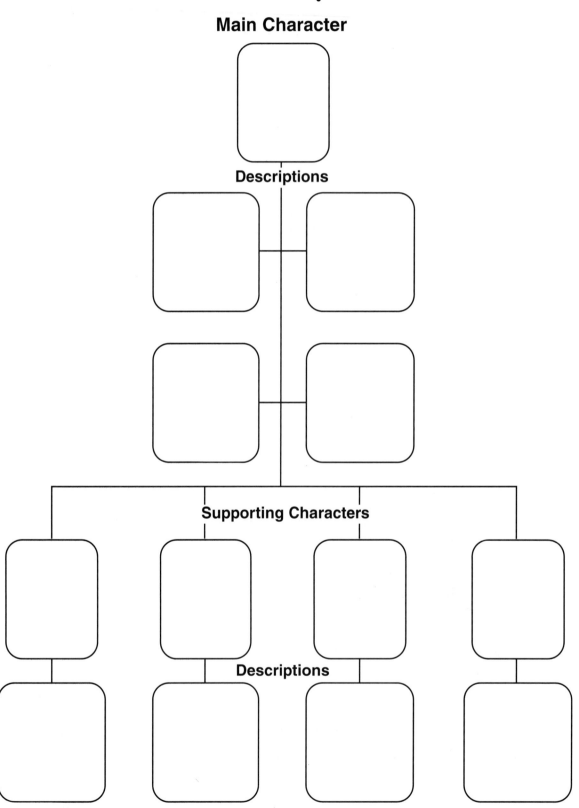

Descriptions

Supporting Characters

Descriptions

Story Pyramid

Book Title

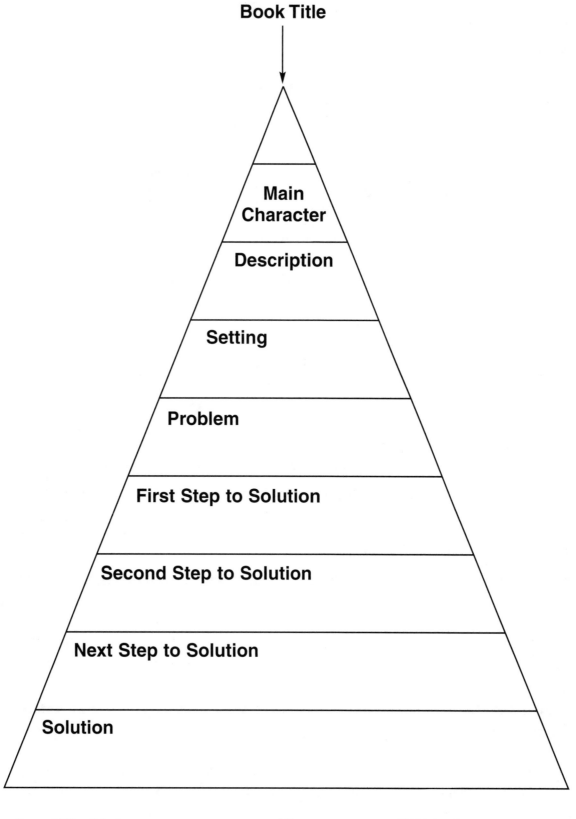

Main
Character

Description

Setting

Problem

First Step to Solution

Second Step to Solution

Next Step to Solution

Solution

Graphic Organizer Activities *(cont.)*

Character Biography

Standards: 5.2, 6.5

Students use this graphic organizer to analyze a story character.

Materials

- children's books
- pencils
- copies of the Character Biography Organizer (page 155)

1. Explain to the students that they will analyze a story character in as much detail as possible, depending on the information provided in the story.
2. Each student selects a children's book and identifies the main character.
3. Distribute copies of the Character Biography Organizer (page 155) to complete.
4. The student writes the character's name, approximate age, and where he or she lives.
5. Then the student records three personality traits, three of the character's actions, and three things the character likes or dislikes.

Analogy Organizer

Standards: 5.2, 6.3, and 6.5

This organizer encourages critical thinking.

Materials

- children's books
- pencils
- Analogy Ideas (page 157)
- copies of the Analogy Organizer (page 156)

1. Teaching your students to make analogies is probably easier to do by providing demonstrations such as:

> *bib* is to *baby* as *napkin* is to *adult*

2. Explain that a baby uses a bib to keep clothes from getting dirty, and an adult uses a napkin for the same reason.
3. Provide the students with the following example:

> *house* is to *person* as _____ is to *bird*

4. Allow the students to offer suggestions. Then draw their attention to the fact that a person lives in a house and a bird lives in a nest.
5. Then distribute copies of the Analogy Organizer (page 156) to each student. Explain that they will complete analogies related to selected stories and characters. (See page 157 for analogy ideas.)

Character Biography Organizer

Character Name

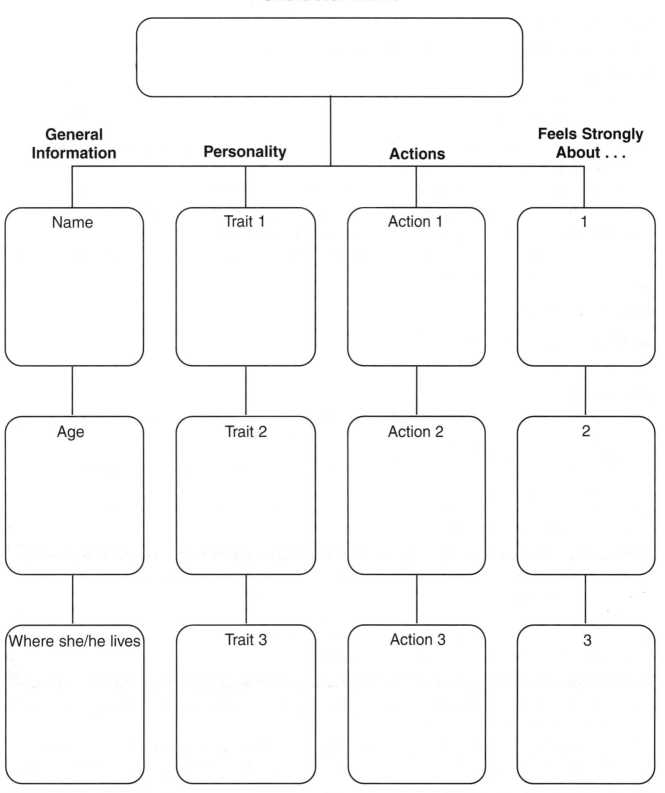

General Information	Personality	Actions	Feels Strongly About . . .
Name	Trait 1	Action 1	1
Age	Trait 2	Action 2	2
Where she/he lives	Trait 3	Action 3	3

Analogy Organizer

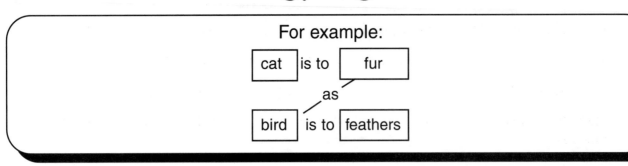

For example:

cat | is to | fur

as

bird | is to | feathers

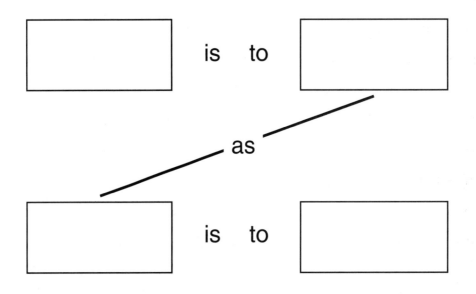

is   to

as

is   to

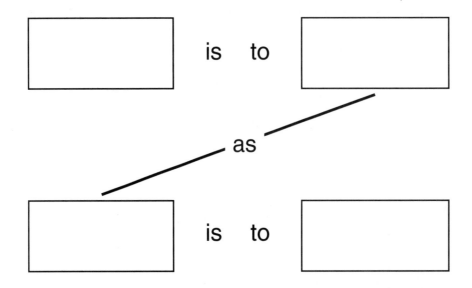

is   to

as

is   to

Analogy Ideas

1. [Personality trait] is to [character] as [different personality trait] is to [different character].

2. [Home] is to [character] as [different home] is to [different character].

3. [Action] is to [character] as [different action] is to [different character].

4. [Character's sibling] is to [character] as [different character's sibling] is to [different character].

5. [Character's parent] is to [character] as [different character's parent] is to [different character].

6. [Age] is to [character] as [different age] is to [different character].

7. [Hobby] is to [character] as [different hobby] is to [different character].

8. [Dislike] is to [character] as [different dislike] is to [different character].

9. [Author] is to [book] as [different author] is to [different book].

10. [Hair color] is to [character] as [different hair color] is to [different character].

11. [Problem] is to [character or story] as [different problem] is to [different character or story].

12. [Best friend] is to [character] as [different best friend] is to [different character].

13. [Good deed action] is to [character] as [different good deed action] is to [different character].

Create some of your own analogies below.

_____ is to _____ as _____ is to _____ .

_____ is to _____ as _____ is to _____ .

_____ is to _____ as _____ is to _____ .

_____ is to _____ as _____ is to _____ .

_____ is to _____ as _____ is to _____ .

_____ is to _____ as _____ is to _____ .

_____ is to _____ as _____ is to _____ .

_____ is to _____ as _____ is to _____ .

Graphic Organizer Activities *(cont.)*

Sphere of Influence

Standards: 5.2, 6.3, and 6.5

Students use this graphic organizer to delve into the events of a story.

Materials

- chart paper
- marker
- copies of the Sphere of Influence organizer (page 159)
- pencils
- children's story

1. Explain to students that a person's actions influence other people or events. For example, if you say something rude to someone, you influence that person by hurting his or her feelings. This can also have an effect on others. (See the example below.)

> Boy is rude to a classmate.   Classmate's friends feel badly for him.
>
> Boy is rude to a classmate.   Classmate's parents are upset that the child is sad

2. Draw a sphere of influence (see page 159) on chart paper. Use the book *Alexander and the Terrible, Horrible, No Good, Very Bad Day* by Judith Viorst as an example.

3. In the center of the circle, write "Alexander's brother is mean to him." The remainder of the sphere could be completed as follows:

> **Direct Influence:** Alexander is upset.
>
> **Secondary Influence:** Alexander has a bad day.
>
> **Distant Influence:** People around Alexander are affected by his feelings.

4. Distribute copies of the Sphere of Influence organizer (page 159).

5. Instruct students to complete the organizer using a character and an event from a selected story.

Venn Diagram

Standards: 5.2, 6.3, and 6.5

This graphic organizer is used to compare characters in a story.

Materials

- chart paper
- marker
- copies of the Venn diagram organizer (page 160)
- pencils
- children's story

1. Explain to the students that they will compare characters in a story.

2. Draw a Venn Diagram on chart paper.

3. Label the center section Both. Label each of the outer circles with a different character's name.

4. Ask the students to tell personality traits that relate to one or both of the characters and write these traits in the corresponding areas of the diagram.

5. Distribute Venn diagrams (page 160) to the students and allow them to complete the diagrams with two other story characters.

Sphere of Influence

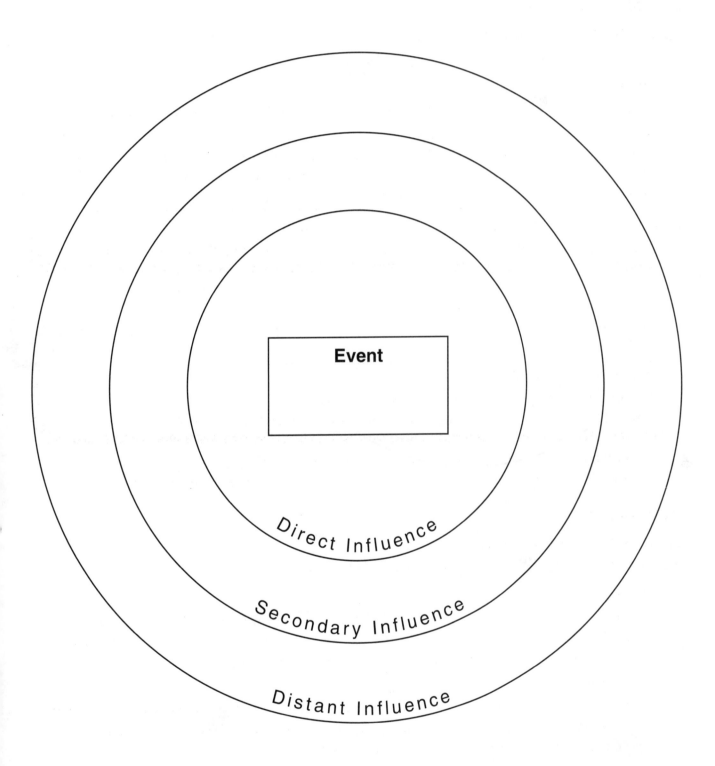

Venn Diagram

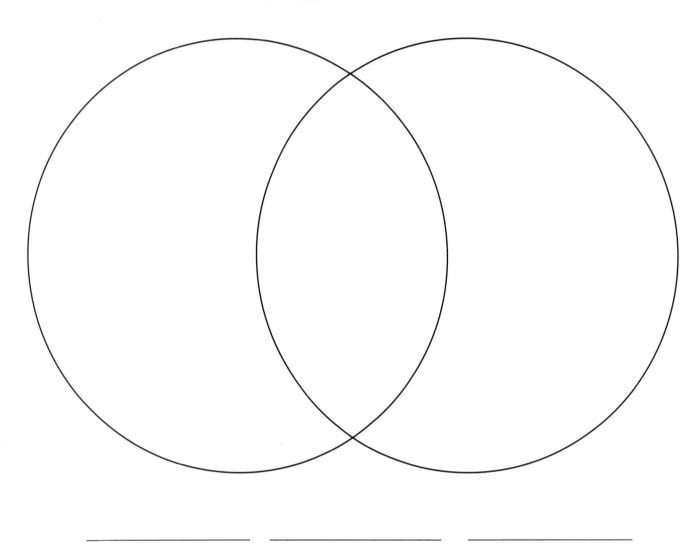

_____   _____   _____

Character   **Both**   **Character**

Answering Questions Activities

Questioning Strategies

Questioning students about their understanding of a story is something most educators do, but the kind of questions asked is extremely important. Some questions only require students to repeat information, while other questions require students to think critically. The list below provides questioning strategies and discussion starters you can use to effectively monitor students' comprehension.

Knowledge
- What events do you recall from the story?
- What traits do you remember about the main character?

Comprehension
- Describe the story setting.
- Compare two characters in the story.
- What is the main idea of the story?

Application
- What conclusion can be drawn about . . .?
- What evidence is given about . . .?
- Why do you think the character did that?
- Write an example of . . . .

Analysis
- What do you think will happen next?
- What causes that to happen?

Synthesis
- Design a plan for . . . .
- Develop a way the character could . . . .
- Construct . . . .
- How could we solve the character's problem?
- What would happen if . . .?

Evaluation
- What do you think?
- What is your opinion?

Question Formation

Standards: 5.9, 6.6

Use the organizer on page 162 to assist children in generating questions.

Materials
- copies of page 162
- pencils
- children's books

1. Distribute a copy of page 162 to each student. Discuss each type of question.
2. The student writes the title of the book in the center.
3. Then the student writes a question for each section on the organizer.
4. Encourage students to pair up to ask and answer questions.

Question Formation

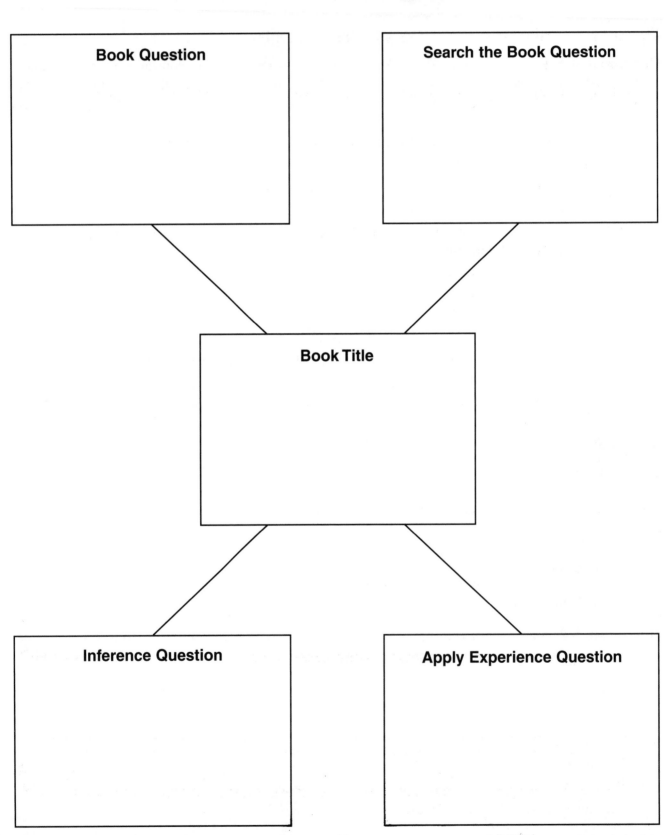

Book Question

Search the Book Question

Book Title

Inference Question

Apply Experience Question

Generating Questions Activities

Character Questioning

Standards: 5.9, 6.5

This activity will enhance students' comprehension by giving them the opportunity to ask questions.

Materials

- chart paper
- marker
- children's literature books
- paper
- pencils

1. Ask your students to think of characters featured in a book they recently read.
2. List these characters on chart paper.
3. Ask the students to think about one of the characters on the list and what they would ask that character if given the opportunity.
4. On another sheet of chart paper, write that character's name. Then ask the students to offer questions they would like to ask.
5. List these questions below the character's name.
6. Next, instruct each student to select a book to read.
7. As the student reads, have him or her think of questions to ask the main character. Instruct the student to write these questions on paper.
8. Finally, have students meet in pairs to share their questions and brainstorm possible answers the character might have.

Dreams of the Future

Standard: 5.9

Use this activity to help your students generate questions.

Materials

- paper
- pencils

1. Ask your students to think about dreams they have for the future, such as:

- places they would like to go
- careers they would like to have
- hobbies they would like to do
- things they would like to learn to do

2. Divide the students into pairs.
4. Then have each student make a list of questions to ask his or her partner about this dream. For example:

- How long have you wanted to do this?
- Why is this interesting to you?
- What steps will you take to do this?
- Do you think this dream will come true?

5. Have the partners meet together again to ask and record their questions.

Generating Questions Activities *(cont.)*

The activities below help students generate questions and refer to Standard 5.9.

Stranger Interviews

Materials

- children's story
- copies of page 165
- pencils

1. In this activity, students will ask and answer questions as if they were characters in the story.

2. Begin by having students read the same story. Ask the students to imagine that they were able to be in the setting of the story, observing (but not participating in) the story events.

3. Ask the students: "Which events do you think were interesting? Which events or actions are confusing? Is there one character that is particularly interesting to you? What questions would you like to ask this character? What questions would you like to ask other characters in the story?

4. On page 165, have each child write questions to ask a character of choice.

5. Once students have completed their question sheets, invite them to volunteer to be selected characters in the story.

6. Instruct a student to pretend to be a character as another student asks questions from his or her sheet.

7. Encourage the student in character to answer the questions as if he or she is really that character. See the example below from *Charlotte's Web:*

   Interviewer: Charlotte, why do you like Wilbur so much?

   Charlotte: He is so innocent and has a good heart.

   Interviewer: Does Wilbur ever frustrate you?

   Charlotte: Yes, he does. He is always so worried.

Hot Seat

This activity quizzes students to answer details about a story.

Materials

- large chair
- children's story
- list of questions (prepared by students)

1. To play, one student is selected to sit in the "hot seat" at the front of the room.

2. Students take turns asking comprehension questions about the story (prepared in advance).

3. The student in the hot seat earns points for answering correctly.

Comprehension Game

Standard: 5.9

Materials

- copies of pages 166–167
- game markers
- index cards
- children's story

1. Have each student create a game with questions about a particular story. 2. The student assembles the game board (pages 166–167) and then writes questions on the index cards relating to the story.

3. Ask students to share their games with classmates to test their comprehension.

Interview Questions

Name of Character: _____

Questions about the character's actions:

1. _____

2. _____

3. _____

Questions about how the character feels:

1. _____

2. _____

3. _____

Questions that challenge the character's actions or decisions:

1. _____

2. _____

3. _____

Additional questions:

1. _____

2. _____

3. _____

Comprehension Game

Directions for two players:

1. Place a game marker on START.

2. Player 1 draws a card and answers the question.

3. If correct, the student moves ahead one space.

4. If incorrect, the student does not move ahead.

5. Player 2 draws a card and answers the question.

6. Continue in the same manner.

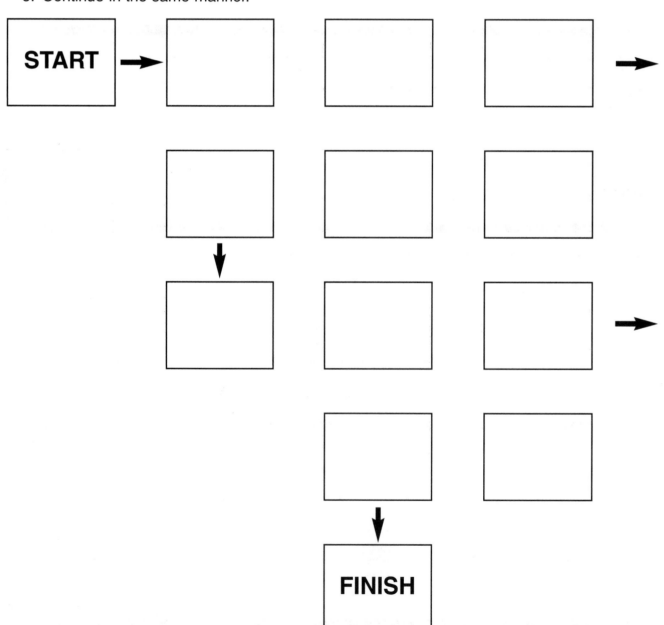

Comprehension Game *(cont.)*

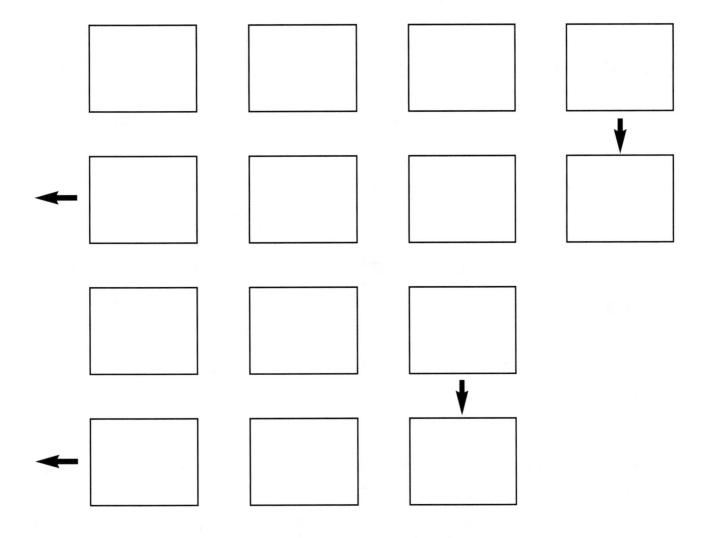

Summarizing Activities

Summarizing Information

Standard: 7.5

This activity helps your students summarize information.

Materials

- paper
- pencils

1. Begin by asking each student to think about a movie he or she has recently seen.
2. Ask, "If someone asked you to tell about the movie, would you tell every single detail that happens?"
3. Point out that when we tell a shortened version of what happens, we are giving a *summary*. A summary only covers the most important parts of the story.
4. Explain that a summary includes the main idea of the story and a few important details.
5. Instruct each student to write a story about a recent event. This story can have as much detail as desired.
6. Divide students into pairs and have them read their stories aloud to each other.
7. Instruct each partner to write a summary of the story using just a few sentences (no more than four).
8. Have the partners share their summaries and compare the summaries to the original stories.

Morning Summaries

Standard: 7.5

This daily routine helps students summarize information.

Materials

- paper
- pencils

1. Begin a daily sharing routine by inviting a few students to share a story or event with the class.
2. The classmates should listen carefully to each student's story.
3. Ask the students to summarize the information using just a few sentences. Remind them that the summary should include the main idea of the story and a few important details.
4. Each day, allow a few different students to share; then have their classmates write the summaries of other jstories.

Summarizing Activities *(cont.)*

Summarizing Stories

Standard: 7.5

Summarizing is an important skill for students to learn and it reflects their comprehension.

Materials

- chapter book
- chart paper
- marker

1. Explain that when reading a story, a person encounters a lot of information. To tell someone about the story, we summarize the information.

2. Review with the students that summarizing means telling the most important events that happen.

3. Explain that when summarizing, it is not necessary to mention all of the details; only the important facts are needed. A person can always refer to the original text if he or she wants to know all of the details.

4. Read aloud a chapter of a book.

5. Ask the students to think of the main events.

6. Invite students to name these events as you list them on chart paper.

7. Ask the students to read through the list and then identify the sentence that represents the main idea.

8. Circle the main idea sentence.

9. Next, explain that when telling the main idea we should use our own words. This is called *paraphrasing*.

10. Assist the students in creating a paraphrased summary of the chapter.

Techno-Summaries

Standard: 7.5

Allow students to apply their summarizing skills using information on the Internet.

Materials

- computer with Internet access
- copies of page 170
- pencil

1. Locate an appropriate Web site of interest and display it on your classroom computer. (Select a site that contains stories or articles for children.)

2. Explain to the students that they will spend time locating interesting articles or stories to read.

3. Distribute a copy of page 170 to each student.

4. Explain that the page is to be completed using information from the selected article or story.

5. Remind them to use what they know about summarizing and paraphrasing to complete the page.

Techno-Summaries

Name of Web site:_____

Name of Story or Article:_____

Events or Important Facts:

1. _____
2. _____
3. _____
4. _____
5. _____
6. _____
7. _____
8. _____

Main idea sentence:

_____

_____

_____

Two supporting events or facts:

_____

_____

_____

Paraphrased main idea (use your own words):

_____

_____

_____

Comprehension Chart

Track student progress by recording comments about comprehension several times throughout the year.

Student: _____   Date: _____

General Comprehension:

_____

_____

_____

Answering Comprehension Questions:

_____

_____

_____

Generating Comprehension Questions:

_____

_____

_____

Using Graphic Organizers for Comprehension:

_____

_____

_____

Understanding Story Structure:

_____

_____

_____

Summarizing:

_____

_____

_____

Additional Comments:

_____

_____

_____

Self-Assessment

Answer the questions to check your comprehension as you read a story.

1. What is the title of the story?

   _____

2. Who are the most important characters? Write their names and brief descriptions.

   _____

   _____

   _____

3. Where does the story take place?

   _____

   _____

4. What part of the story first grabs your interest?

   _____

   _____

5. Which character in the story has a problem? Describe the problem.

   _____

   _____

6. How is the problem resolved?

   _____

   _____

7. How does the story end?

   _____

   _____

8. List two questions that you have about the story line or the characters.

   _____

   _____

9. Summarize the story using four sentences or less.

   _____

   _____

   _____

   _____

Answer Key

Page 21
1. must
2. zoo
3. fix
4. leap
5. sharper
6. frown
7. candle
8. keep
9. cheater
10. chatter
1.–5. Answers will vary.

Page 27
1. bat
2. rain
3. wake
4. say
5. peel
6. keep
7. ten
8. yell
9. tent
10. best
11. still
12. ring

Page 29
1. ten
2. box
3. went
4. truck
5. gift
6. lunch
7. cat
8. dig
9. lock
10. bed
1. tip or top
2. pat, pit, pot, or put
3. mod or mud
4. dig or dog
5. trap
6. pat, pet, pit, or put

Page 30
1. key
2. flute
3. ice
4. cake
5. coat
6. rain
7. pea
8. goat
9. bike
10. cane

Page 31

t	table	kitten	carrot
l	leather	smelly	tell
f	fine	baffle	stuff
m	more	hammer	tram
b	bread	dribble	cab
p	patch	happy	jeep
g	gentle	digger	hug
n	never	windy	heaven

Page 33

Hard Sound	Soft Sound
gave	gentle
cupboard	gel
give	gem
giggle	gym
goal	gypsy
gobble	cellar
gush	cent
guppy	citizen
cabin	cycle
cotton	cement
custard	city
cobbler	cyclone

Page 38
Answers will vary.

Page 41
1. prize
2. front
3. dry
4. friends
5. cream
6. trick
7. dream
8. great
9. present
10. train
11. cried
12. gravy

Page 42
1. flag
2. play
3. blocks
4. clown
5. plant
6. planet
7. slipper
8. sled
9. glass
10. clock
11. flute
12. blanket

Page 43
Answers will vary.

Page 44
1.–9. Answers will vary.
1. trunk
2. plant
3. sink
4. hand
5. shelf
6. stand

Page 45

2. fry	long "i"
3. family	long "e"
4. silly	long "e"
5. sky	long "i"
6. gypsy	short "i"

Answer Key *(cont.)*

7. cycle — long i
8. many — long e
9. cherry — long e
10. gym — short i

Page 46
1. th
2. ph
3. wr
4. ch
5. gh
6. wh
7. sh
8. kn
9. ck
10. gn
1. mother
2. knife
3. chalk
4. wrong
5. wheel
6. share

Page 47

Beginning	Middle	End
ship	benches	rough
write	orphan	graph
they	telephone	much
know	brother	brush
why	other	earth
gnaw	tickle	sick
chirp	birthday	tough

Page 51
1. I am — a
2. is not — o
3. you are — a
4. do not — o
5. let us — u
6. it is — i
7. we will — wi
8. I have — ha
9. was not — o
10. are not — o

Page 52
1. we're
2. aren't
3. they'll
4. it'll
5. couldn't
6. you're
7. he's
8. don't
9. can't
10. I've
11. she'll
12. wasn't

Page 53
1. taller
2. shorter
3. youngest
4. biggest/bigger
5. fatter
6. oldest
7. wider
8. smallest

Page 54

1. faithful	faithless	X	X
2. X	X	illness	X
3. X	X	sadness	sadly
4. colorful	colorless	X	X
5. X	X	slowness	slowly
6. X	X	sickness	sickly
7. helpful	helpless	X	X
8. thankful	thankless	X	X
9. X	X	neatness	neatly
10. X	X	loudness	loudly
11. careful	careless	X	X
12. painful	painless	X	X

Page 55
1. skipped — skipping
2. hopped — hopping
3. batted — batting
4. begged — begging
5. dripped — dripping
6. stopped — stopping
1. smiled — smiling
2. baked — baking
3. filed — filing
4. voted — voting
5. tuned — tuning
6. named — naming

Page 59
The Green Leaf

sea	long "e"
leaf	long "e"
floating	long "o"
said	short "e"
green	long "e"
boat	long "o"
took	short "u"
would	short "u"
soaked	long "o"
you	long "u"
clean	long "e"

Toad on a Road

cheerfully	long "e"
road	long "o"
glorious	short "u"
exclaimed	long "a"
leaves	long "e"
beautiful	long "u"
believe	long "e"
season	long "e"
took	short "u"
seat	long "e"
air	long "a"
meal	long "e"
continued	long "u"

Page 60
1. seat — meat
2. soap — boat
3. rain — pail
4. tie — lie
5. blue — glue
6. bean — jeep

7. coat   float

8. mail   claim

9. tried   cried

10. tail   bait

11. team   heat

12. fried   tried

Page 61

1. soon	7. book
2. soon	8. book
3. book	9. soon
4. soon	10. soon
5. soon	11. book
6. book	12. soon

Page 62

1. enjoy
2. drew
3. toy
4. blew
5. boy
6. coins
7. out
8. how
9. house
10. found
11. few
12. owl
13. oil
14. down
15. boil

Page 64

1. not fair
2. not agree
3. read again
4. not favor
5. not true
6. wrap again
7. not certain
8. not able

9. not obey
10. load again
11. not like
12. not sure
13. not even
14. do again
1. unhappy
2. unmade or remade
3. dishonest
4. uncaring
5. rebuild
6. unopened or reopened
7. refill

Page 67

1. one		6. our
2. bee		7. right
3. won		8. eye
4. write		9. I
5. hour		10. be

Page 117

1. Slang—lemme

   Let me see what's happening.
2. Slang—wassup

   Tim, how are you?
3. No slang
4. Slang—gotta

   Please help me with my homework.
5. No slang
6. Slang—gonna

   I'm going on a trip next week.
7. Slang—gimme

   Give me the toy, please.
8. Slang—like

   That was so much fun!
9. No Slang
10. Slang—chill out

    Don't get upset. Just calm down.

Page 132

1. act		5. shame
2. bow		6. wiggle
3. trust		7. glad
4. place		8. cuff

Page 133

Answers will vary.

Page 134

Answers will vary.

Page 139

Causes

1. I ate too much pizza.
2. I slipped on the ice.
3. The grass was long.
4. It snowed.
5. My dog was hungry.
6. I forgot to water the plant.
7. I sprinkled food into the tank.
8. I won the game.
9. Sally cut her finger.
10. I helped my dad clean the garage.

Effects

1. I have a stomachache.
2. I bruised my hand.
3. My dad mowed the grass.
4. Everything was white.
5. My dog whined.
6. The plant died.
7. Fish came to the surface.
8. I screamed.
9. Sally cried.
10. My dad was happy.

Page 142

1. Fact		6. Opinion
2. Fact		7. Fact
3. Opinion		8. Fact
4. Opinion		9. Opinion
5. Fact		10. Opinion

Page 172

1.–9. Answers will vary.

References

Fiction

Gardiner, John Reynolds. *Stone Fox.* HarperCollins, 1980.

Howe, Deborah and James. *Bunnicula.* Simon & Schuster, 1979.

Kellogg, Steven. *Can I Keep Him?* Puffin, 1992.

Lewis, C.S. *The Lion, the Witch, and the Wardrobe.* HarperCollins Juvenile Books, 2000.

Munsch, Robert. *Pigs.* Annick Press, 1992.

Numeroff, Laura Joffe. *If You Give a Mouse a Cookie.* Laura Geringer, 1985.

O'Dell, Scott. *The Island of the Blue Dolphins.* Houghton Mifflin, 1990.

Sharmat, Marjorie Weinman. *Gila Monsters Meet You at the Airport.* Scott Foresman, 1990.

Spinelli, Jerry. *Maniac Magee.* Little Brown & Company, 1999.

Van Allsburg, Chris. *Jumanji.* Houghton Mifflin Co., 1981.

Viorst, Judith. *Alexander and the Terrible, Horrible, No Good, Very Bad Day.* Aladdin Library, 1987.

Williams, Vera B. *A Chair for My Mother.* HarperTrophy, 1984.

Nonfiction

Center for the Improvement of Early Reading Achievement (2001). *Put Reading First.* US Department of Education.

The National Reading Panel (2000). "Teaching Children to Read: An Evidence-Based Assessment of the Scientific Research Literature on Reading and Its Implications for Reading Instruction—Reports of Subgroups."